Praise for

HIGH-STAKES LEADERSHIP
and CONSTANCE DIERICKX

"Constance Dierickx takes you on a journey through courage that starts with your intellect, enters your heart, and refreshes your soul. **High-Stakes Leadership** is the alchemy that combines smarts, guts, and courage that produce brilliance, a quality not in great abundance in business today. What struck me most is that all of us are in high-stakes businesses, but too many of us act as if we can succeed in some safe zone. Constance pulls away the safety net and teaches us how to soar."

—Alan Weiss, PhD, author of *Million Dollar Consulting,*
Lifestorming (with Marshall Goldsmith), and over 60 other books

"Constance Dierickx illustrates high-stakes leadership with stories of leaders who exemplify key leadership qualities of courage, judgment, and fortitude. I'd add another quality to this list: Her leaders show a degree of grace that is uncommon in the business world. These examples, backed by research, show what makes a leader great during turbulent times."

—Daniel H. Pink, author of *Drive and To Sell Is Human*

"Constance is the only person I know who transitioned from a stockbroker to a psychologist. Perhaps that is why her insights and advice are so relevant and pragmatic. I deeply appreciate her insight and wise counsel which she captures in this book."

—Walt Rabe, PE, President and Chief Executive Officer,
Schnabel Engineering

"**High-Stakes Leadership** is straightforward, uncomplicated, and full of real world examples that illustrate the qualities that distinguish great leaders. Especially valuable are the stories of leaders who made mistakes or failed before achieving success. Constance shows us that the right attributes help leaders learn, face reality, dust themselves off, and snatch victory from the jaws of defeat."

—Bob Lamm: Co-Chair, Securities and Corporate Governance Practice, Gunster, Yoakley & Stewart, P.A.; Independent Senior Advisor, Deloitte Center for Board Effectiveness

"Constance Dierickx's *High-Stakes Leadership* informs, entertains, and most of all teaches timeless lessons. Her pragmatism and deep knowledge of behavior are a powerful combination and will add lasting value to the reader."

—Katherine Jackson, PhD, former Chief Technology Officer, Westinghouse

"Constance combines strategic thinking and pragmatic advice in a way I find absolutely unique. She asks difficult questions that need to be asked. Her qualities and style come through clearly in *High-Stakes Leadership* making it a valuable guide for executives responsible for major changes with far reaching consequences—high-stakes situations."

—Colin Boyd, Chief Information Officer, Komatsu Mining Company

HIGH-STAKES
LEADERSHIP

HIGH-STAKES LEADERSHIP

Leading Through Crisis with Courage, Judgment, and Fortitude

CONSTANCE DIERICKX, PHD

bibliomotion
inc.

First edition published in 2018
by Bibliomotion, Inc.
711 Third Avenue New York, NY 10017, USA
2 Park Square, Milton Park, Abingdon, Oxon OX14 4RN, UK

Bibliomotion is an imprint of Taylor & Francis Group, an informa business

No claim to original U.S. Government works

Printed on acid-free paper

International Standard Book Number-13: 978-1-138-08860-3 (Hardback)
International Standard eBook Number-13: 978-1-315-10974-9 (eBook)

This book contains information obtained from authentic and highly regarded sources. Reasonable efforts have been made to publish reliable data and information, but the author and publisher cannot assume responsibility for the validity of all materials or the consequences of their use. The authors and publishers have attempted to trace the copyright holders of all material reproduced in this publication and apologize to copyright holders if permission to publish in this form has not been obtained. If any copyright material has not been acknowledged please write and let us know so we may rectify in any future reprint.

Library of Congress Cataloging-in-Publication Data
Names: Dierickx, Constance, author.
Title: High-stakes leadership : leading through crisis with courage, judgement, and fortitude / Constance Dierickx.
Description: New York : Taylor & Francis, [2017] | Includes bibliographical references and index.
Identifiers: LCCN 2017010330 (print) | LCCN 2017010928 (ebook) | ISBN 9781138088603 (hardback : alk. paper) | ISBN 9781315109749 (ebook)
Subjects: LCSH: Leadership. | Crisis management.
Classification: LCC HD57.7 .D554 2017 (print) | LCC HD57.7 (ebook) | DDC 658.4/092—dc23
LC record available at https://lccn.loc.gov/2017010330

Visit the Taylor & Francis Web site at www.taylorandfrancis.com

Printed and bound by CPI Group (UK) Ltd, Croydon, CR0 4YY

Contents

Contents

Acknowledgments

I wish to extend my deepest thanks to colleagues, friends, and family for their encouragement and support. I especially want to thank my clients, past and current, who work earnestly to add value, make the tough decisions, and do the right thing.

The colleagues with whom I learn, collaborate, and explore are among the finest consultants and people I have ever met:

Linda Henman, PhD, dear friend and wicked smart colleague, who supports, pushes, and makes me laugh until my sides hurt.

Linda Popky, excellent writer, marketer, and loving Jewish mother to everyone in her purview.

Alan Weiss, PhD, who has taught me more about consulting than I ever thought possible and without whose insistence I would not have written this book. He once called me a "fearless learner." I am inspired to live up to that description.

Frank Ricker, my grandfather. I was lucky to grow up with so much of his influence. I learned by hanging around his office, eavesdropping on business conversations, and watching him spot opportunities in the marketplace in our small town. If anyone was a fearless learner, it was he.

Robert Cialdini, PhD, excellent researcher and expert on influence. I use his research daily and cannot recommend his books highly enough. He graciously spoke with me to help me integrate his research with the ideas in this book.

Peter Economy and Mark Levy, who helped me formulate my ideas and get them written.

I thank, too, the many leaders with whom I spoke for this work. Some are named while others preferred anonymity. Each has a lesson from which we can all learn.

Michael Dierickx, Amy, and April, for making my life more interesting, meaningful, and fulfilling than I would have ever dared hope. Eric and Lance, who are the reasons I say, "We hit the son-in-law lottery!"

Preface

High-stakes leadership. The phrase has a ring of drama, and for good reason. When risk and ambiguity are both high, leadership can make the difference between success and failure.

This book offers a series of examples of leaders and organizations that exemplify courage, judgment, and fortitude when the stakes are high. Some of the leaders highlighted are well known, while others are relatively unknown outside their own spheres. Some of the organizations—The Home Depot, Best Buy, and Reckitt Benckiser—have market capitalizations in the billions, while others fly below the radar of most of us. The parallels between these well-known companies and the lesser known ones are, nonetheless, real and robust. The lessons from Frank Blake, former CEO of The Home Depot, resonate in the stories of the Girl Scouts of Western Washington and Schnabel Engineering.

Indeed, the risks faced by smaller organizations may be more threatening than similar risks faced by larger concerns. The CEO of a $40 million company considering a $5 million acquisition can't make a mistake. A larger company may do a deal of similar magnitude, miss the mark, and yet survive. The CEO in each case will suffer some loss in terms of reputation, and investors and employees will be impacted as well. A larger company, however, has more protections against risk and actual losses.

While leaders of large organizations are advantaged in some ways, their network of constituents is larger, and these leaders are never far from the spotlight. Many who masquerade as "advisors" to top leaders are actually pursuing an agenda other than the best interests of the leaders and their business. It takes discernment to know the difference. Leaders who have such discernment are extraordinary. Those without it default to habit or hibernation, neither of which works, except temporarily.

Successful leaders in 2017 are dealing with issues that we could not have fathomed a mere fifteen years ago. Each opportunity and each risk comes with a host of tactics, methods, technologies, and slogans and represents bandwagons upon which many will leap. This is not leadership, no matter the fancy language or clever packaging. Leading requires the courage to make conscious decisions about what to do, the judgment to separate information from short-term trends, and the fortitude to remain true to oneself and one's mission. In so doing, leaders are also teachers. They teach by example, often without realizing it. The essential aspects of good leadership endure even as the environment and tactics change. Indeed, courage, judgment, and fortitude are not merely tools for survival, they are the means by which we can sculpt the future.

INTRODUCTION

Some years ago, Bart Becht was named CEO of Reckitt Benckiser, an organization formed through the merger of two global companies, Reckitt & Colman and Benckiser. Becht knew that, in addition to merging global operating units and functions, he would need to bring together the cultures of each company. He would need to meld the corporate cultures, yes, but also ethnic cultures.

Becht has many talents. One that is pivotal is his ability to establish a direction and simplify the path to get there. He has the courage to accept risk, let people try things, and remove whoever or whatever stands in the way. He does the equivalent of removing drag from an aircraft's skin, streamlining it in the process. No matter how much fuel you have, you aren't going to get where you want to go if you're dragging too much baggage. Bart Becht doesn't allow on his plane people who bring too much baggage.

The combination of courage, good (not perfect, *good*) judgment, and fortitude worked for Becht. The share price of Reckitt Benckiser doubled in two years—a nearly unheard-of feat. Under Becht's leadership, the company went on to make other acquisitions and grow market share, create new products, and increase operating profit and revenue at a pace that far outstripped the increase in the company's employee population.

What is it that makes some leaders—leaders like Bart Becht—so successful, while others fall so very short? I believe that today's most successful leaders are expert practitioners in something I call *high-stakes leadership*—the ability to lead effectively in times of whitewater change and great risk. As John Kotter says, "Rate of change in the world today is going up . . . fast, and it's affecting organizations in a huge way."[1] In my experience, some leaders are able to deal with all this change and risk, and some are not.

High-stakes leadership does not require you to be a special person or have unnatural powers. Nor must you necessarily be in a dangerous situation or in a tremendously risky environment. High-risk leadership is described in a simple, three-part model that is accessible to anyone—at any level in any organization, big or small. The model illuminates the mind-sets, strategies, and tactics used to make tough decisions, take an unpopular stand, or ignore convention, and it provides readers with a practical template for action (see Figure 0.1).

The model's first element is *courage*. Courage gives us the ability to act with clarity and focus. It grounds us and provides important information upon which we can make decisions. Without courage, decisions are made on the basis of tradition, habit, or whim, or are made in a purely reactive mode. As a leader, if you don't have courage, you are lost.

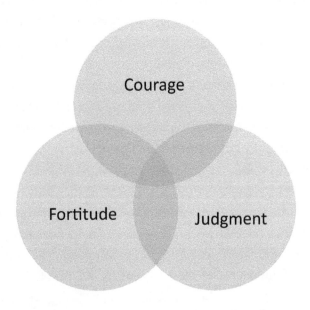

Figure 0.1 *Courage, Judgment, Fortitude*

Decisions made on the basis of habit are the antithesis of strategic. This is precisely why strategy must be clear and vibrant. Leaders can look to strategy to help them make decisions. They can point to it so that others understand why particular decisions are made, and on what to base their own decisions. This is always important, but it is especially critical in a time of transition. For example, when a leader leaves an organization, discussions often start with, whom? This is the wrong question. The right question when preparing to fill the leadership gap is, for what purpose?

When I began working with a large trade association a couple of years ago, the board was clear about the threats to their survival (they were facing the same problem as many other associations—declining membership) but unclear about their direction. They were flailing, and they knew it. We agreed that job one for the new CEO would be to create a strategy. They hired a brilliant man to lead the organization, but within ninety days, they were threatening to fire him. Why? What went wrong? The CEO and the senior management team created a strategy that the board objected to. Actually, worse than that, board members were threatening the CEO and one another. There were out-and-out verbal battles, threats, and predictions of dire consequences. This organization's operational focus dwarfed its sense of direction. The group survives today, though it is much smaller and far less influential.

The model's second element is judgment. Judgment forces us to test ideas using reason, and it demands course corrections and even retreat. Without good judgment, you run with an idea whether it's good or not. Reckless judgment will take you off the tracks.

Long before Amazon was the huge company it is today, Jeff Bezos was criticized for his judgment. He was investing heavily in a company without profit, and allowed himself to be filmed riding around a warehouse on a toy while showing off his memorable laugh. He was mocked. People raised eyebrows and wondered if this guy could make it happen. Results aside for the moment, Jeff Bezos trusted his own judgment. He was clear and committed to the course he had laid out, and he didn't let anyone else knock him off this path. Jeff Sonnenfeld, a noted commentator on governance, said, "Someone on the board needs to help this guy. He looks bad." Sonnenfeld was sincere in his advice, and no one in the audience argued with him. In hindsight, it seems Bezos's judgment has been stellar. High-stakes leaders trust their judgment. While they aren't blind to input, they maintain a healthy disregard for feedback and consensus.

The model's third and final element is fortitude. Fortitude is a renewable source of energy that's needed to accomplish great tasks. It helps us be resolute and inspires others to continue even when they have doubt. Absent fortitude, good ideas and plans become yesterday's news.

When Capt. Kristen Griest and 1st Lt. Shaye Haver—both graduates of West Point—entered the Army Ranger program, many doubted their ability to finish successfully. Women had never done this before.[2] The program was grueling—both physically and mentally. The women made news, however, when the two of them completed the program. But they didn't just complete the program. A stunning testimonial from a male colleague made it clear that Lt. Haver had fortitude to spare. Michael Janowski, 2nd Lt., reported that, while on a grueling training march, he was carrying a particularly heavy load. He asked his colleagues for help, but only one stepped forward. That person was Lt. Haver. Janowski said, "She literally saved me. I probably wouldn't be sitting here right now if it weren't for Shaye."

The fortitude it took for Haver to do what she did is remarkable, but Ranger Janowski knows something about fortitude as well. Twice before he had been dropped from the Ranger School as he fought testicular cancer, which had progressed to stage IV. The third time was the charm, however, and through great personal courage and fortitude, he achieved his goal.

Whether one needs physical, psychological, mental, or moral fortitude, great achievements are rarely accomplished without it.

In this book, I draw from my more than twenty-five years of experience working with high-stakes leaders like Bart Becht in companies ranging from start-ups to large, global organizations. I also draw on the latest scientific research on courage, judgment, and fortitude to provide you, the reader, with an objective lens through which you can view the topic.

I hope you enjoy reading this book as much as I enjoyed writing it. Now more than ever, we need leaders who are willing to step up in these risky, fast-changing times.

Notes

1. John Kotter, "Can You Handle an Exponential Rate of Change?" July 19, 2011, accessed February 20, 2017, www.forbes.com/sites/johnkotter/2011/07/19/can-you-handle-an-exponential-rate-of-change/#309e4d5a1f6f.
2. Mark Thompson, "America: Meet Your First Female Rangers," August 20, 2015, accessed February 15, 2017, http://time.com/4005578/female-army-rangers/.

CHAPTER 1

High Stakes

When a donor wrote a check to the Girl Scouts of Western Washington for $100,000, it was a joyous day for CEO Megan Ferland and her team. This donation was nearly one-third their annual budget.

Ferland and her colleagues knew this money would help send to camp girls who otherwise could not go. It would help the Girl Scouts extend membership to girls who may not have another place where they felt included and were encouraged to learn, grow, and feel the priceless sense of pride that comes from accomplishment.

Then, one day, Ferland received a letter in which the donor made a very specific request: "Please guarantee that our gift will not be used to support transgender girls. If you can't, please return the money."

This sort of exclusion is antithetical to what the Girl Scouts is all about. And while the situation might have presented a difficult dilemma for some leaders, Ferland says she didn't even need to think about it.

What did Ferland do? She returned the money. It was clear to her that the organization could not keep the money. She said that Girl Scouts is "for every girl." Her purpose was clear, and her judgment allowed her to understand immediately that agreeing to this untenable restriction was not an option. So, she returned the check.

Ferland's actions offer a sterling example of high-stakes leadership. Despite the risk to her organization of returning a $100,000 contribution, Ferland's deep well of courage, good judgment, and personal fortitude led her make the right decision for the Girl Scouts of Western Washington. A lesser leader might have caved, deciding to compromise the organization's core values in exchange for the contribution.

What happened next, however, was nothing short of stunning. Ferland and her team went public with their decision. Then, they launched a fund-raising campaign on Indiegogo. Next, they created a compelling video about what Girl Scouts is about. They didn't attack the donor, though many saw this person as a bigot. Rather, the video is a touching message about young girls and why Girl Scouts is so important.

The story spread like wildfire. When I saw it, I immediately posted about the story on Facebook. I was calling out to my friends, some of whom grew up with me in Cocoa Beach, Florida. Several of us were in Girl Scouts together from age seven through high school. A few had joined the eight hundred thousand adult volunteers now involved. More than a few Chevrolet Suburbans were sold to these dedicated women so they could take troops of Girl Scouts on trips.

Ferland and her team tapped into a potent resource—women who have an emotional connection to their time in the Girl Scouts. *Fifty-nine million women and girls are in, or have been in, the Girl Scouts.* I am one of those fifty-nine million, and my memories of camping, canoeing, and hiking the Appalachian Trail endure. Memories are great, but skills, resourcefulness, and resilience are even better.

As a Girl Scout, I learned how to tie fancy knots and when to use each type of knot. I learned how to stabilize a broken bone, whether the fracture was closed or compound. We learned how to play guitar, use dry bamboo to create a musical instrument, and sing our way through fear, sadness, or a minor epidemic.

Just imagine—twenty-four teenage girls camping together for two weeks. Primitive camping, nothing sissy! Set up near a beautiful mountain stream, we had plenty of clean water, but it was cold, so cold you wanted to scream when you stepped into it. We took matters into our own hands and decided to make a shower. We had a plastic bucket we could poke holes in but nothing else that would remotely resemble a shower. Undeterred, we used twigs tied together with twine to make a floor. Then, we added more twigs and twine to fashion "walls" that were tied to trees. Finally, we hung a door that swung on hinges made from . . . you guessed it, twine. The work of making this shower took focus, knowledge, and perseverance. Our counselors neither interfered nor discouraged us. They watched and then celebrated with us when we succeeded in making it work.

We grappled with issues from bugs to burrs to bears, and in the end, we succeeded. What was happening to us, besides acquiring knowledge, was that we were developing self-confidence. Underneath the collective sense of pride in our accomplishments, our individual capacities for learning, adaptation, and self-reliance were growing rapidly. The Girl Scouts helped us to be brave, make good decisions, and persist in difficult circumstances. When faced with a problem, or even danger, we didn't crumble.

When I heard about Megan Ferland and the stand she was taking, I was exhilarated. She was acting with boldness and principle, and she immediately became a person of extreme interest to me. Ferland was smart to use the wave of attention to benefit Girl Scouts. She made good use of the platform she had—indeed, she built it as surely as my friends and I had built our shower in the woods all those years ago.

The thought that someone would deliberately interfere with any girl having experiences like those my friends and I had made me furious. I challenged my friends to donate to the Western Washington Girl Scouts. My grassroots plan may have helped. What helped more was the courage of Megan Ferland and the boldness she and her organization used to get the word out. Thousands saw the beautiful video they created for their fundraising effort.

Watching a video, reading the story, and getting mad was one thing. More than seven thousand people did far more—they opened their wallets. In just three days, the Western Washington Girl Scouts received more than $250,000. That's $150,000 more than the donor took back. Ultimately, the one-month Indiegogo campaign raised a total of $338,282.

For many organizations, the loss of $100,000 would be like letting go of a business unit. The donation's return represented a major loss of revenue for the organization. Yet, it fueled efforts to replace the lost revenue, and in this case, what was unleashed produced a significantly higher dividend.

Megan Ferland showed her high-stakes leadership stripes in her decision to turn down money with strings attached. She did something that many leaders of far larger organizations are loath to do—she let go of money because to keep it would have exacted a much higher cost. It would have required that she and her team ignore their principles.

This type of courage is no accident. Ferland is an exceptional person, but she is not alone; the Girl Scouts benefits from the example and legacy of another high-stakes leader, Frances Hesselbein. Originally an adult volunteer in Pennsylvania, Hesselbein rose to become CEO of the Girl Scouts, a position she served in from 1976 through 1990. She transformed the organization during her fourteen years in the role, and Peter Drucker famously said she could run any company in the United States.

Hesselbein brought to the Girl Scouts a clarity of mission that had become obscured before she took her role as CEO. When directing a team to redesign the *Girl Scout Handbook*, she said, "When any girl opens the handbook I want her to see herself."[1] She went on to say that she meant the books should appeal to a girl on a Navajo reservation or a girl in a New England home with a picket fence. That is courage, judgment, and fortitude in action. Frances Hesselbein and Megan Ferland both helped the Girl Scouts by being bold enough to bring these elements together.

Direction

When we think about crisis, we generally think only about the negatives that crises tend to bring with them. A crisis is, after all, a disruption of the calm that we may have enjoyed for some period of time. But one thing a crisis has over calm is that it is extremely clarifying. A fire, flood, or threat of harm focuses people immediately. Objectives, and thus direction, become very clear: survive, reduce discomfort, remove risk, or protect reputations.

As you read this book, chances are you aren't in a crisis. That's the good news. The bad news? Your current lack of crisis can lull you into settling for obscure objectives.

When I ask an executive about the direction in which she wants to go, she usually responds with something like, "I want a strategic planning retreat." I ask why. Not only do we need a "why," we need a "why" that is good enough to justify the investment. If you don't get to the "good enough why," you might have a meeting based on the sole objective of having a meeting. It is the leader who must establish direction, not a meeting planner. The higher the stakes, the more important it is to have clarity about your objectives. Great leaders are firm about what they want to do and are flexible, even innovative, about how they want to do it. The likelihood of success, especially when the stakes are high, is reduced by rigidity.

When Patrick Brennan took the job of leading the integration of Manheim Financial Services (MFS) and Dealer Services Corporation (DSC) after Manheim (an auto auction company now part of Cox Automotive) bought DSC in 2012, his boss gave Brennan very clear direction. Joe Luppino, the chief financial officer at Manheim, said to Brennan, "If one and one does not equal more than two, this will be a failure. Go make it work."

He didn't need to tell Brennan that the way to do it was to add value to customers. That is how Brennan thinks and is a key reason he was put in the role in the first place. The stakes were high because this was a significant acquisition for Manheim, and growing the business would give the company momentum. Failure would mean lost opportunity, revenue, market share, and reputation. The decision about who should lead the merger was important, but Luppino is no stranger to risk. He embodies the characteristics of courage, judgment, and fortitude that a leader needs to successfully navigate when the risks are high. Because mergers and acquisitions are notoriously difficult and fail somewhere between 50 and 80 percent of the time, it was critical to have a good leader overseeing the integration.

Right away, Brennan began to think about the marketplace and strategy. His first concern was to bring together parts of the business in a manner that would have obvious and immediate benefit to customers. This is an extremely atypical approach. Usually, a company starts looking for the mythical "synergies," most of which fail to deliver what people believe or hope they will. Encouraged by run-of-the-mill advice on mergers and acquisitions, many companies start planning how to bring various functions together before they have a clear rationale for doing so. Technicians go to work to weld the pipes without concern for which pipes they are welding, why, or in what order. Overconfidence leads to a false belief that the analysis and due diligence work done before the deal and the pipe welding done afterward will create success. If this were true, more deals would deliver the promised value. A leader who has the courage to be thoughtful rather than mechanical, uses his own experience and judgment, and has the fortitude to focus on the big picture is far more likely to be successful.

Beacons

Leaders who provide a succinct and vivid description of the direction the company needs to go have far greater influence than those who speak only of profit. Their words and actions provide a beacon, reminding people where they are and shining a light on the path they are to follow. No matter the situation, the path can easily become littered with misunderstanding, rumors, and pressure from various constituents. Leaders must provide a beacon that is, in the words of Frances Hesselbein, "as constant as the North Star."

As distracting as lack of clarity is for people inside an organization, the effect on customers is even more profound. When attention is drawn inward, customers take a back seat. Often, this happens without intention or awareness. The realization hits after results sag. Leaders who let customers suffer because the organization's focus is on the wrong things will see erosion in the very part of the market that is most valuable—the part they already have. Ironically, some leaders spend millions to capture new customers while ignoring current customers.

Yet, some leaders abdicate their responsibility to provide the clear and shining beacon that people need. Even if leaders sometimes say, "we don't know yet," that is preferable to gossip and misinformation. Patrick Brennan knew that water cooler talk was inevitable, but he also knew that it could not be a substitute for communication from him and other leaders. To maintain focus, he made decisions at the strategic level with a few key people, keeping them out of the hands of technicians. He focused on the question, how will our customers be better off? Explaining decisions within that frame of reference helps employees understand the changes being made and gives them confidence that the leader knows where he is headed. It takes fortitude to resist the urge to turn mergers and acquisitions integration into a mechanical exercise depicted by colorful slides with timelines and charts. Many a deal goes south because the details are buttoned up, but they are the wrong details.

Customer Value—Tomato, Toe-Mah-Toe

If you had asked a Manheim vice president and a DSC vice president in 2012 what customers want, each would have told you a different story. The vice presidents and general managers of the Manheim auto auctions talk a lot about relationships. They are very good at this, and it gives them important information about their customers. They are interested in the answers to questions such as, what is happening in a customer's business, how can Manheim help, and are there red flags indicating that the customer may have some struggles? The customers of MFS were accustomed to a highly personalized level of service. Some of them had been working with specific individuals within the company for years. Customers trusted these individuals, and to them, MFS was embodied in a single person.

DSC customers interacted with the company in a different way. They used the phone, spoke with a person who visited their dealership, and utilized a web-based system to transact business. In 2012, DSC made a version of its software available for mobile devices. At that point, customers could manage their accounts anytime from anywhere. This was huge!

While MFS and DSC both provided financing, and each placed tremendous importance on customer satisfaction, they pursued their goals in very different ways. The story of DSC, MFS, and the company it became—NextGear Capital—is a case study in mergers. This one has been a stunning success. Why?

- **Leaders showed courageous patience.** Patrick Brennan, the Manheim executive responsible for the integration, has a sense of timing that is rare. He neither rushed in nor used a generic, "weld-the-pipes-together" approach. Brennan moves fast when things are clear and slows himself down when he needs to understand a complex issue. This is a vital characteristic of a high-stakes leader.
- **Customer value and experience were the top priorities.** Understanding customers was critical—the team asked, what do they value? Bart Becht says it best, "At the end of the day, what counts is not what the ten people in that room think, it's what the consumer thinks." His statement is emblematic of another characteristic of a high-stakes leader—a wide lens.
- **The company was sincere with employees.** Leaders who are aware that fear is distracting, and that sharing fears breeds rumors, will act differently from those who assume that employees will merely "go along." Generic approaches do not work. You must identify your best people and hold them close. Those who you do not believe are a good fit need to know that. They need information and help so that they may leave with their dignity intact. None of this will happen if you do not know your employees well. Accurate judgment about people depends upon understanding them. When the stakes are high, there is no substitute for informed judgment.

It's Not Rocket Science

As clarifying as a high-stakes transition or crisis may be, a mission can be equally motivating and can provide great insights for leaders in all arenas. On May 25, 1961, President John Kennedy announced that the United

States would put a man on the moon by the end of the decade. This was an audacious goal. Some thought it foolish or impossible—or both. But the goal clearly exemplifies high-stakes leadership. The risk was high, and there were many unknowns. It took courage to put a stake in the ground, judgment to say that scientists could do it, and fortitude to stay the course.

As a kid in Cocoa Beach, Florida, I knew how important the space program was to our country, and feeling part of it was a thrill. The business of our town was the space business. We were just a few miles south of Cape Canaveral, and our heroes were test pilots, astronauts, physicists, and engineers. The town had a mission. We were clear about it, and whether you worked in the space program or not, many people were affected by the program and found a way to participate.

We watched launches, walking to the beach from school to witness many. When rockets blew up, we were sad. When astronauts were launched into orbit and returned home safely, we cheered. When test pilots and astronauts died, the whole town mourned. It felt personal.

Returning to earth from the early flights meant landing in the Atlantic Ocean in a capsule that was retrieved by helicopters and ships. Once on land, the astronauts would return to Cape Canaveral, riding in slow-moving parade of convertibles. Hundreds of families lined Florida State Road A1A, waiting to see these living heroes. The space race was not abstract for us, it was real.

President Kennedy gave us clear direction. He gave the entire country a sense of mission. Indeed, each NASA project is called a *mission*. This is no accident. The thousands of people who work on a project and support the project are on a mission. They have clarity of purpose that emboldens them. This boldness shows courage and makes others courageous. Great leaders have the ability to lead big missions and find ways to make themselves as visible as the astronauts were to a generation of kids growing up around Cape Canaveral.

While the leaders of NextGear weren't launching rockets, the outcome of their decisions would impact thousands of people. They felt the weight of this and did things to make themselves visible and available for conversation.

This tactic was especially useful given Patrick Brennan's calm and reassuring manner. He was able to help people feel less anxious by his manner, even when he couldn't honestly answer some of their questions.

One thing that Brennan did was insist that every operations leader at Manheim visit the NextGear headquarters. They met all the leaders, toured the facility, and heard from people about their business model, technology, plans for the future, and how they would help customers transition to a different way of doing business with NextGear.

NextGear doesn't launch rockets, but they did something similar to what President Kennedy did when setting the nation's goal to land humans on the moon. They made the direction clear. Then they brought together the people who would implement a new way of operating. When leaders shine a light on the future, people can direct their energy toward getting there.

Simplicity

People need to know why they are doing what they are doing. A clear direction and freedom to move toward it are the two things motivated people need if they are to apply their talent and will.

Recently, I asked a senior executive about the strategy of his small consulting firm. He spoke for nearly twenty minutes. At the end, he was breathless, and I had no more idea about the strategy than when he'd started. This man is neither dim nor inexperienced, despite how this sounds.

He is unable to simplify and, not surprisingly, neither can his colleagues. They have created a culture that uses complicating as a stalling tactic. Not deliberately, but with the same result.

Think about the direction of your company. Does the direction:

- Provide a framework that guides decisions?
- Describe a future state?
- Help you make investment decisions?

If you answer no to any of these questions, you have some simplifying to do before any high-stakes decisions can be made with confidence.

Judgment

Judgment tempers the energy that many think is synonymous with courage. Without judgment, courage can devolve into reckless action. Counterintuitively, when fortitude meets courage, the result can lead to disaster if judgment has no influence.

Judgment is neither gut instinct nor only pattern recognition. Judgment is part experience, part discipline, and part knowledge.

Consider the example of Constance Fletcher. At eighty-three years of age, she is still an artist, and just as sassy as can be. I was in her studio one morning with my canvas set up on an easel. Sunlight streaming through the very large windows made this a perfect spot. Fletcher positioned herself behind me so she could see everything I was doing. She said, "Paint."

I painted. Then she said, "Paint some more." After a few lines were on the canvas, she started teaching. She used what I had done as the content for the lesson. I painted, she commented, and then I did more.

Fletcher did not judge what I had done. She didn't ask why. This was both freeing and terrifying. I had only impulse to go on. I lacked both the knowledge and experience to make decisions based on judgment. Despite my usual love for trial-and-error learning, I desperately wanted to know, before I put paint to canvas, what it would look like.

Then, Fletcher told me something important. She said, "Learn the rules first. Then, later, when you break them, you'll know what you are doing." Her way of teaching was very experiential. It was a Montessori art class just for me. Do something, and then learn about what you did.

The rules can be used to understand principles, as she explained, or to restrict. In art, you don't want restriction unless you are copying. The principles can be applied to produce an endless number of outcomes. Whether the artist chooses harmony or discord, the choice is a judgment. Judgments are made according to your own vision.

Leaders have a similar challenge. They know some rules but don't know exactly what will happen. When and how will what they know intersect in a particular context? What looks good in one scenario can play out very differently in another.

Artists and leaders need to use judgment to take action. Then they must observe the effect and make another judgment. Sometimes, Fletcher told me, you must abandon your work. I was struck by this because it isn't an easy thing to do. When we make an investment in a piece of art or a business, we can become very attached to it. The concept of sunk costs applies both to business and to art. The idea is that, once we have made an investment that feels significant to us, we have a hard time letting go. Yet, an artist may need to put a canvas aside to free up energy for another project.

In business, we often hang on to unproductive plans, people, or entire businesses long after it is clear we should cut them loose. Why? Because the human urge is to preserve that in which we have invested. Sometimes the most expeditious act is to divest. Let go. Free up your mind, energy, money, and talent to pursue something else.

Fear of Judgment

Ralph Waldo Emerson once wrote about foolishness, consistency, and those with little minds. If only his words could influence the legions of people in organizations who put their energy toward means rather than ends. Leaders cannot allow allegiance to method to be mindlessly maintained.

Helen, the head of human resources for a $20 billion company, was railing against the mindless people in her organization. I told her of the issues in the fastest-growing part of the company. Number one? Talent. "We can't hire great people because HR won't let us!" was the cry from the leadership and managers.

When I told Helen this, she erupted. "The salary guidelines are *guidelines!* What is wrong with these people?" Interesting question, since, as the leader of the function, she is responsible for "these people." Further, it was notable that until the business leaders started screaming, she wasn't so concerned about the rigid application of guidelines.

Leaders who build their organizations around rules rather than judgment will ultimately fail. Why? Because they are looking at how well people follow rules, not how well they think. To think is to make judgments, have opinions, and give them voice. Fear of being wrong or criticized prevents many from speaking up. Yet, not doing so gives more room for the reckless actors. Volume is not a great criterion for credibility, but it trumps silence.

One of my most influential teachers was Dr. Don Turner, a psychiatrist in Atlanta, where I attended graduate school. Dr. Turner asked me if I liked something. My answer was too long-winded for him to buy it, and he spotted my equivocation. He said, "It's an easy answer—like or don't like. No thought required. Not answering is avoidance." It seemed so simple and, yet, clarifying. Once you answer that question, you can think about why.

While working with a chief executive officer a few years ago, I recognized his reluctance to make judgments. I was curious about why every effort to grow the company had failed. It became clear when I asked him a seemingly unrelated question about his head of business development. He had no idea neither how much business he had brought in nor the value of any partnerships he had initiated. Absent this information, he felt paralyzed to do anything about this person who was, to be blunt, a major pain.

Fear of making judgments is rooted in fear of holding people accountable. If I follow the rules, then you can't blame me. If I don't know and can't find out, then you can't blame me. If I don't know how to evaluate you, then I don't have to face the hard truth that you aren't adding value. This is no position for a leader. It will, however, lead to crisis.

Courageous Judgment

If you're a leader, there isn't always time to gather all the information you want. Still, you have to make a decision. How do you do that?

Leaders use what is known as *pattern recognition*. People in all walks of life use it, but those who are successful do it extremely well. What are they doing? Matching an element from one environment or person to what they have stored in memory. For example, every time I meet prospective clients, they ask me a series of questions. The person's questions, tone of voice, and mannerisms tell me whether we are building rapport or not. That is pattern recognition, which I use to make a judgment.

Marcus Lamonis, an entrepreneur and star of the television show *The Profit*, does a brilliant job of making judgments. He has seen a lot of businesses. His memory bank of businesses, business models, leaders, processes, and the look and feel of businesses tells him a lot. Furthermore, that memory bank helps him determine what needs further investigation.

Lamonis takes businesses that are on the brink of failure and turns them around. That is his purpose. Once he is interested in the business idea, he makes a judgment about the owners. He will work only with people who respond well to his style of unvarnished truth telling. He makes judgments based on criteria he knows are important, and he delivers them in a very clear manner.

If Lamonis shied away from making judgments, he wouldn't enjoy the success he does. And neither would the people he has helped become successful, enjoy their vastly improved financial situations, and lead more peaceful lives.

Once a business owner agrees to work with Lamonis, the stacking of the deck begins to change. Lamonis is the owner's partner, not his competitor.

The dividends are financial, yes. But the owner also makes revolutionary improvements in self-esteem, confidence, and peace of mind. Lamonis helps businesses, and he changes lives in the process. Watch an episode of the show and see his genuine glee when his partners do well. He is proud of them. Even better, he is proud *for* them. He understands the value of helping people realize their own capacity and then rise to fulfill it.

Key West Pie Company is a small business on the southernmost tip of the Florida Keys. Key West is an iconic place where Ernest Hemingway hung out and bathing suits are considered appropriate attire for most activities.

When Lamonis first began working with the pie company, things were in a mess, with financial strain, owners in conflict, and little discipline in the company's processes.

Then, there was Tami Forbes. Forbes was the very essence of chief cook and bottle washer. She ran the operation, figuring out how to do things she'd never done before and using very good judgment in the process. Lamonis spotted her smarts and dedication right away. Within a very short time, Lamonis bought out the owners and put Forbes in a position to use her talent and rewarded her accordingly.

The result? Forbes was instrumental in turning the business around. She thrived with the support of someone who believed in her and provided support. In a wonderful update to the TV segment on Key West Pie Company, we see Forbes again. As she spoke with Lamonis, she had a glow. She described new products, sales growth, and the joy of working in the company. Her enthusiasm was heartwarming. Lamonis was equally thrilled with the change in the business and delighted to see Forbes doing so well.

Marcus Lamonis's judgment was spot on. He didn't overlook Tami Forbes, something many would have done. The payoff? Financial gain, yes. But the payoff for Forbes was literally life changing. Though she is no longer with the company, Forbes, in working with Lamonis, affirmed her own strengths and learned valuable business lessons that will endure.

Fortitude

Without fortitude, a leader may be successful in the short run, but her success won't last. When a leader is doing anything ambitious, barriers of all sorts are a given. Leaders who lack determination and resilience may give up or change course too easily.

One leader who knows about obstacles and fortitude is Lance Ledbetter. In the late 1990s, Lance could be found in the control room of the student-run radio station at Georgia State University in Atlanta. The station's reputation for edgy music and unscripted commentary has kept it on the air for decades.

Ledbetter, who was a graduate student at the time, was also a disc jockey at the station. One of his gigs was a gospel music show on Sunday mornings. Ledbetter wasn't happy playing only the tried and true—he wanted to hear music that was hard to find. By definition, if something is hard to find, it's hard to find. Lance began contacting record collectors and asking them about their collections. He read voraciously about the history of music and recordings. He discovered collectors who had thousands of records, some with storage units piled high with boxes of unorganized albums. Others, like Joe Bussard, had rooms filled with records and could lay their hands on exactly the one they wanted at a moment's notice.

These collectors didn't necessarily trust this young man or his intentions. Ledbetter invested time and money in getting to know them and letting them see that he had great respect for their efforts to gather and keep safe music that is important.

When the *Anthology of American Folk Music* was released, Ledbetter had to search for a copy. Finally, he connected with a local person who could sell him a copy. They met in a parking lot and exchanged the set for cash. Ledbetter said, "It felt like a drug deal."

The process of discovering rare music is both frustrating and exhilarating. Trips down back roads in rural towns mixed with travels to Greenwood, Mississippi, for the Robert Johnson Festival; a week at a Shape Note Music Camp in Alabama; and conferences in Raleigh, North Carolina, Nashville, Tennessee, and Los Angeles, California.

Ledbetter wondered if others would be interested in this music. He decided to take a gamble and launched a project to document, digitize, and package a collection of rare gospel music.

The effort took him five long years. The resulting box set was entitled *Goodbye, Babylon*, and Ledbetter released it under the label he founded, Dust-to-Digital. When it was released, he was deep in debt. Ledbetter says he thought a few hundred copies of the set would sell. Then he would get a job, get on with his life, and pay off the debts.

Goodbye, Babylon was nominated for a Grammy Award in the Best Historical Album category, and a set made its way into the hands of Bob Dylan, who bought copies for his friends. Dust-to-Digital's reputation generated a lot of interest from collectors, musicologists, curious listeners, and academics.

It took five years of focus, sweat, worry, and just plain guts to create one project. Today, Lance Ledbetter is internationally known for his thought leadership and curatorial talents. Dust-to-Digital, Ledbetter, and his wife, April, have to date garnered more than ten Grammy nominations. In 2008, Ledbetter won a Grammy for Best Historical Album for *The Art of Field Recording, Volume One*. Winning is nice indeed but, as important, Ledbetter is a standard bearer of excellence in his realm and someone others seek to emulate.

Optimism

It's interesting that some people look upon the success of others and feel defeated. Another's success means less opportunity for them—they view success as a zero-sum game. Some, however, look at the success of others and say, "Now I know it's possible." The defeatist attitude of the former group is a way to avoid risk and is the antithesis of fortitude.

Fortitude requires resilience. It's about finding ways around things as much as enduring them. It's about seeing obstacles as temporary and seeing ourselves as capable agents in our lives rather than helpless. This is how Martin Seligman describes optimism. He says we can learn to be more optimistic. I'd add, we can learn to be more resilient.

Seligman's book *Learned Optimism* is a great contribution to psychology and to humanity. In this book, he describes several key aspects of optimism.[2]

- **Permanence.** When bad things happen, I see them as temporary.
- **Pervasiveness.** When something goes wrong, I see a specific cause. Instead of saying "College is useless," I might say, "That course was useless."

- **Personalization.** I can take credit when I do something well. Conversely, when things go wrong, I can see how external factors may have played a role in the outcome.

If we believe that the success of others comes from luck, we can't replicate it. If believe in our ability to learn and adapt, we may learn from others who have done what we wish to do.

The Guts to Give Up

Growing a business involves attracting and acquiring loyal customers, great employees, superior suppliers, and more. It also takes letting go of things and people that are not adding value. Letting go of what doesn't work is like throwing useless baggage off an airplane in flight—it lightens the load and allows you to get where you want to go. Too much junk in the trunk can slow even a Ferrari.

I have learned from working with successful people that they don't focus only on where they want to go and having the fuel to get there; they intentionally get rid of things that create drag. It is very common for leaders to tolerate drag of all sorts, failing to recognize the downside. Why? It can be harder to stop doing something than to add more to the list. Human beings see the impact of something when it occurs all at once more easily than we see cumulative effects.

General Electric (GE), under the leadership of Jack Welch, famously got rid of businesses that were not top in their sector. It may not have been easy to implement that part of the strategy, but compared with individuals giving up bad habits and leaders admitting to bad decisions, GE's jettisoning of businesses was much more straightforward. Even so, getting rid of things that aren't working is not easy in an organizational culture where there is neither history nor habit of doing so.

The tendency for even very smart leaders to hang on to bad investments, for example, is not reason to question their intelligence. Such behaviors are a feature of being human, though it's one we should monitor—mostly in ourselves.

Universal Leader

When Pope Francis became the head of the Catholic Church, we had no idea how this man would change the way the church is viewed. His actions have drawn the attention of millions of people, many of whom are not Catholic.

When a young boy approached him during a service and wanted to stand with the pope, Francis embraced him. He held the boy's head in his hands and kissed him, not allowing others to escort the boy away. The warmth, calm, and genuineness of this leader have captivated us.

While the images of Pope Francis greeting people with love and sincerity were early signs of his ability to influence, we were soon to see this as only a part of the way he leads. John L. Allen Jr., associate editor of the Crux website, writes that this pope is like "shock therapy" for the church.

Allen is right that Pope Francis is shaking things up, but many would not use the word *shock*. Why? Because the reasons for Pope Francis's decisions seem to be based on his belief that all people are important and worthy of care. His focus is on inclusion, not condemnation. His conduct is exemplary, and his refusal to accept royal treatment may shock traditionalists, but it makes him more human to the rest of us.

The images of the Pope in his modest little Fiat are certainly memorable. The sight of him stopping his motorcade, while visiting the United States, to speak with a disabled child and his family is heartrending. To do these things, which are so kind, he must argue with those who are trying to protect him. They see danger, and for good reason. Undoubtedly, there is someone, somewhere, who wishes to harm him. Yet, he chooses to be vulnerable so that he can pursue his vocation and mission.

This is not naïve, as some suggest. It is brave.

Unhappy Endings

As it happens, Volkswagen (VW) has been embroiled for many months in a huge legal and public relations mess. The company has admitted to installing a so-called defeat device—software that allows it to dupe emissions tests—on millions of diesel-powered cars. After this cheating was revealed, VW's CEO resigned, and the company is planning a massive recall. The estimates of how many vehicles are involved keep climbing; first, it was a few thousand, but the number is now reported to be as many as eleven million.

Soon after the emissions scandal hit the news, Autotrader reported a drop of more than 1 percent in the price of used VW vehicles and more than 3 percent for diesel vehicles. The VW Beetle diesel and Jetta diesel both showed declines in the average list price of more than 4 percent. This equates to $1,110 for the Beetle and $797 for the Jetta. VW doesn't take a direct hit on these cars because they are in the secondary market, having been sold directly by VW only when they were new. But every individual or dealer attempting to sell one of these cars now has an asset that is worth less than it was just a month before the revelations. Think these folks are angry at VW? You bet. What the leaders at VW do in response to this crisis is critical.

The case at VW brings up an important point. Usually, when people think about dishonest employees, they think about theft and greed. They think about people trying to get something by stealing.

A far greater risk is employees who are protecting something. What would that be? It could be stock price, credibility with customers, or confidence of bosses. It needn't be something so tangible. It might be the reputation of an individual or a company.

VW engineers, especially those at the top, have excellent reputations. Falko Rudolph, the head of a components factory near Kassel, Germany, was chief of Volkswagen's diesel-engine development for four years, beginning in 2006. He is credited with being the father of the company's dual-clutch transmission, and is widely admired. He was also part of the team of engineers that developed the EA 189 diesel engine, which is the engine at the center of the emissions scandal.

Did this lead them to commit dishonest acts? I don't know. But I do know that it wouldn't be the first time people acted to protect their status. The damage to VW has just begun to be visible. As top leaders grapple with reality and work to address both the crisis and underlying systemic issues, conflicts are erupting.

One of the company's longest-tenured and most successful executives abruptly resigned. In 2015, fifty-eight-year-old senior executive Winfried Vahland was appointed CEO of a new organization that would bring together the U.S., Canadian, and Mexican operations. However, before reporting to his new post, Vahland abruptly resigned from VW. The Dow Jones news service reported that Vahland was in conflict with other leaders over strategy and organization decisions at VW.

Losing talented people who participate in egregious acts is harmful. Losses of talent from the fallout are even more damaging. Key to recovering from a disaster is top leaders who are trustworthy and aligned. VW's issues will linger far longer if credible leaders can't get on the same page.

The need to be right, to win, or to forge ahead has caused small missteps as well as big disasters.

Unchallenged Thinking

Those who work in the space program have a name for the urge to forge ahead. They call it "go fever."

Who can forget the explosion of the *Challenger* space shuttle? On January 28, 1986, news crews were at Cape Kennedy broadcasting the launch live to the world. We remember the sight of the booster rocket exploding and the look of horror on the faces of those watching as seven astronauts died. A camera caught the mother of Christa McAuliffe. McAuliffe was the first teacher to go on a mission, and sadly, her mother watched as the craft exploded.

Afterward, a thirty-two-month-long halt in the shuttle program put the entire program in doubt. President Ronald Reagan appointed a commission to study the disaster. Astronauts Sally Ride and Neil Armstrong were on the commission, as was Nobel Prize–winning physicist Richard Feynman, who would later recount some of the commission's work in his book *What Do You Care What Other People Think?*

Through the commission's process, we became aware of O-rings and Morton-Thiokol—the name of the defense-contracting firm that built the solid-fuel booster rockets, one of which failed and caused the shuttle to break up. What many don't recall is that Morton Thiokol put the "red line" at forty degrees Fahrenheit, meaning they couldn't say the design was safe below this temperature. The risk from unreliable O-rings was deemed critical, yet despite the importance of this part of the craft and the knowledge of its problems, ultimately the project leaders decided to launch.

The decision to launch was due, in part, to "go fever." The flight had been postponed five times. People were frustrated and the public disappointed. When you are on "the Cape" (as locals call it), or in a nearby town, the tension becomes almost unbearable.

Nevertheless, the day of the launch, with ice all over the launch pad and a crew working through the night to clear the vehicle of ice, the decision was to launch:

> Failures in communication . . . resulted in a decision to launch 51-L based on incomplete and sometimes misleading information, a conflict between engineering data and management judgments, and a NASA management structure that permitted internal flight safety problems to bypass key Shuttle managers.
> —Rogers Commission Report, Chapter V

Richard Feynman was so dissatisfied with the report of the Presidential Commission on the Space Shuttle *Challenger* Accident, known as the Rogers Commission, that he threatened not to sign it. Only when he was allowed to write an appendix, recounting his own observations, did he relent. Known as Appendix F,[3] it is a stunning and clear piece of writing.

Wrote Feynman in the appendix, "For a successful technology, reality must take precedence over public relations, for nature cannot be fooled." Dr. Feynman understood high stakes better than most. As a young physicist during World War II, he worked on the development of the atomic bomb and simultaneously pointed out the flawed security around the facilities where this work was being conducted. He demonstrates an important attribute of high-stakes leadership, that of being pragmatic even while working on a critical and highly technical mission.

Facing the Music

When Mary Barra became CEO of General Motors (GM) in December 2013, she had a lot to say grace over. GM stood accused of using faulty ignition switches that resulted in thirteen deaths.

Just months after Barra became CEO, GM was fined $35 million for failing to recall cars with faulty ignition switches. The National Highway Traffic Safety Administration said the company had allowed the switches to be used for more than a decade, while knowing there was a problem with them.

GM subsequently announced that they are also facing seventy-nine customer lawsuits with $10 billion sought for losses attributed to the recall. As the story unfolded, it became clear that more cars were involved. The total number was eventually set at 2.6 million.

To her credit, Barra stepped up to the plate in a way her predecessors had not. She, and everyone else, learned about the technical reasons for the failures. But she went further to ask why such failures, which were not a secret, were allowed to be perpetuated by GM's engineers and managers. That is a question about culture, behavior, and an atmosphere in which lying was an acceptable practice.

GM has had to come clean about what it had done, but not before people died. NASA has had to deal with the risks that we humans create in systems that are highly technical. Indeed, rocket scientists make them. Still, things go wrong.

At Volkswagen, it seems that some engineers couldn't bring themselves to admit that they hadn't solved the problem of how to improve mileage while lowering emissions in diesel-fueled cars. Instead, they rigged the measurement methods. Thankfully, this did not cause deaths, but it certainly has damaged brand credibility and trust.

Did someone pay the engineers to do this? It doesn't appear so. Why weren't they discovered? Beliefs. The very reputations that these engineers had built prevented others from questioning them. Implausible explanations become believable when the messenger is trusted.

Fortitude Isn't Enough

When I ask people about courage and what they think it is, most respond with a version of, "It's doing things even if you are afraid" or "It's about being bold."

This common understanding about the meaning of courage leads us astray. It doesn't distinguish the truly courageous from those who are merely bold and perhaps rash. It leads us to overuse the word and thus dilute its power.

I developed the model of high-stakes leadership to help my clients better define what they need to bring strategy to life. This is the great gulf in business, the vast space between idea and results. Leaders who are courageous, use good judgment, and have fortitude generate dividends beyond those achievable with only one or two of these attributes.

The people described in the following chapters, whether from the worlds of business, military, or sports, have demonstrated courage. They have each taken personal risks in service of accomplishing something of value—to themselves and others. You, the reader, can learn from the people highlighted in this book.

As with any such endeavor, this book does not shine a light on every high-stakes leader who deserves it. I think of the military personnel whose leadership happens in extremely dangerous circumstances; the women and men who are police officers and firefighters facing high risk and low certainty on our behalf; the brave humanitarian workers who deliberately go into dangerous situations, including war zones; and the medical personnel who leave the safety of their homes to go where deadly disease outbreaks would go unchecked without them. These people, and others about whom we may never hear, are willing to fulfill a mission even when the risks are extreme and the ability to mitigate them unknown and perhaps unknowable. They are high-stakes leaders, and because they exist, others are willing to follow them and perhaps become great leaders themselves—the ability to lead in high-stakes situations can be strengthened. You can develop it yourself using the model described in this book and by using the people as role models. Onward!

Notes

1. Frances Hesselbein, *My Life in Leadership: The Journey and Lessons Learned Along the Way*. San Francisco, CA: Jossey-Bass (2011).
2. Martin Seligman, PhD, *Learned Optimism: How to Change Your Mind and Your Life*. New York: Free Press (1990), pp. 44–51.
3. Richard P. Feynman, "Report of the Presidential Commission on the Space Shuttle Challenger Accident. Volume 2: Appendix F—Personal Observations on Reliability of Shuttle," June 1986, accessed February 15, 2017, http://history.nasa.gov/rogersrep/v2appf.htm.

PART I

Courage

Courage is the first of human virtues because it makes all others possible.

—Aristotle

CHAPTER 2

Courage in Crisis

The word *courage* is laden with emotion and high drama. Just look at its etymology.

"Courage" comes from the Latin *cor*, which means "heart." Heart, in fact, has been used as the defining quality of courage—likely for as long as there have been people on the face of this earth. The proverbs and folktales that we all grew up with are chock-full of examples of brave men and women who faced down very scary circumstances, people, and the occasional monster to achieve their goals.

When someone is bereft, we tell them, "Take heart." When someone shows insight, we say they've cut through the chaos to get to "the heart of the matter." When we have a very honest and in-depth conversation with someone, we are said to have had a "heart-to-heart talk."

This heart part of courage is, of course, essential. But it's not enough. To be courageous, you need more than heart. You need other qualities that are just as important—like direction, judgment, and fortitude.

Courage, then, can be built through the steady application of a specific mind-set and practices. Once established, the mind-set becomes automatic. Rehearsal strengthens people's ability to perform and makes them confident in their ability to do so. These practices make courage more reliable, rather than accidental or reckless.

Perhaps nowhere else is our courage as leaders tested—to its very limits, and sometimes beyond—than when we are dealing with a crisis. In business, a crisis can arrive quite unexpectedly, and in many different forms. A competitor offers a new product that is vastly superior and less expensive than your own. A key employee quits. The server that controls your retail point-of-service system is hacked. Your Dallas warehouse is severely damaged in a hailstorm.

Merely determining the nature and magnitude of a bad situation is not as obvious as it seems. Information comes in packets—sometimes the least important pieces first. Photos and sound bites on TV or websites can make the same event look different depending upon the framing, narration, interpretation, and the information that is shared or left out.

A small thing we notice but ignore can become a big problem. Something we notice and mention to someone else may be important, but what if that person convinces us that it isn't real or material? What if we are told by others that the things we see as signs of danger mean progress?

Historic Courage

In the 1930s in Germany, there were laws introduced called the Nuremberg Race Laws, which placed restrictions on Jewish citizens. Later, Hungary adopted similar laws modeled on those in Germany. Raoul Wallenberg, a Swedish citizen, was traveling to Europe during this time for business reasons. Of privileged background, he was engaged in a business of importing and exporting. His life was easy in Sweden, but he was aware of the dangers growing in Europe. A discontent was growing in Wallenberg, though he was in no personal danger.[1]

Quite unexpectedly, he was asked to go to Hungary as a member of the diplomatic corps. His role was to organize and run a humanitarian department whose mission was to protect as many Jews as it could.

In Budapest, Wallenberg encountered Adolf Eichmann. Eichmann's mission was to round up the remaining Jews in Budapest for deportment, leading almost certainly to their deaths. Eichmann had the power of the Third Reich behind him; Wallenberg had diplomatic status, wits, and courage. This may seem like an uneven match, but Wallenberg managed to save as many as one hundred thousand people in a few short months. So courageous was he that he was known to confront German soldiers attempting to remove people and get them to back down. When the Russian Army marched into Hungary near the end of the war, Wallenberg was rounded up. He was interrogated and determined to be a spy, then sent to a Russian prison, never to be heard from again.

Among those saved by Wallenberg is Tom Lantos, who later served in the U.S. House of Representatives. Mr. Lantos sponsored a bill to make Wallenberg an honorary American citizen, one of dozens of awards given to him since the end of World War II.

Thankfully, most of us will not be called upon for acts of courage that rise to this level of heroism. We can learn from Raoul Wallenberg even though most of us will never face a situation with such high stakes.

Leaders are often lobbied by people who want to persuade them to adopt a particular point of view. The effectiveness of this persuasion depends upon several elements including the person doing it, recent past events, who else agrees or disagrees, and so forth. Absent an obvious, dramatic event, determining if something is a crisis or could become a crisis is less objective than one might think. When the German and Hungarian governments were enacting anti-Jewish laws, there were plenty of people supporting it. In business as well as government there are always people supporting bad ideas and dangerous moves. Leaders who lack the courage to be independent in their thinking aren't leaders at all.

Some leaders develop a reputation for being most influenced by a single aspect of an argument; often, they are swayed either by who makes the argument or if it was the last thing they heard. This doesn't happen because a leader decides to be impressionable. Rather, it happens unconsciously.

How do leaders reduce the effect of irrelevant information or determine when they need more, or better, information? By asking themselves the following questions:

- What am I being told?
- What is the evidence presented?
- What have I observed?

- How does the narrative presented differ from the evidence?
- What information do I need?
- What are the risks of underestimating seriousness?
- What are the risks of overestimating seriousness?

The Light at the End of the Tunnel Is a Train

A large organization with a shiny reputation hired a CEO after a search-and-selection process that took months. The new CEO is one of the smartest men I've ever met. He was visionary, entrepreneurial, and prone to move fast on ideas. The board, recognizing the need for the organization to change, hired him precisely for these attributes. Problems arose, however, seeded in a very common situation. The board was not on the same page about how fast the organization needed to change. They chose the fast-moving candidate without also being ready to deal with the consequences of that choice.

This happens frequently. Usually, given some time and effort to build good working relationships, boards come to an understanding among themselves and with a chief executive. Ideally, the tensions ebb and flow. A healthy board is stuck in neither harmony nor conflict, and deals with both. The selection of a chief executive officer is one of the most important roles of a board, and the process (it should not be an *event*) often causes emotion to rise to the surface or engenders it where none was felt before. It is high stakes for the individuals, the board, the organization, and all its constituents.

The board in this case (which I cannot name for reasons that will become obvious) was frustrated by poor results. The sitting chief executive officer was stuck in the past, a controlling person and as dour as they come. He would resign once a new leader was named. It was no secret that he wasn't happy about his retirement or the limited influence he had on the selection process. The board was sympathetic to him and not unkind, but they didn't let him run the show. Good for them. Nonetheless, he lobbied various board members, sounding the alarm of impending doom if person X was not selected. The chairman of this board had to meet with the CEO and tell him in no uncertain terms to "butt out." It took courage to do this because some of the other board members were not in agreement. It caused a kerfuffle, but the chairman did the right thing.

High-Speed Train on Old Tracks

The new CEO took the role with enthusiasm and high hopes. Most of the board members were equally thrilled. A few were bitter. This division and lack of candor were the seeds of crisis. It took less than three months for the board and CEO to butt heads. It was no secret. The senior staff knew it, and key customers were feeling that something was amiss.

The new CEO did a few things that set him at odds with the board. First, he dug more deeply into the financials and came to some conclusions that he felt should be discussed immediately. Second, he began sharing a very big idea with the senior staff. They were excited *and* terrified. The third thing was not something the new leader did directly. Rather, it was something he failed to recognize. He didn't understand that some of the senior staff had long-standing and close relationships with some board members. There was a grapevine as strong as I've ever encountered, but the new leader ignored it.

Things came to a head when one of the senior executives began talking to a board member about the new CEO. Nothing on its own was all that big, but small things caused the board member concern. Finally, the board member took these concerns to his colleagues who, by now, were feeling quite out of the loop regarding what the new leader was doing from a strategic point of view.

My phone rang. The board was set to hold an emergency meeting and planned to fire the new CEO. "Have you spoken to him about your concerns?" I asked. "No," was the answer. I recognize that the reader will think that either I am making this up or that this has to be the most amateurish board ever convened. Neither is true. These were very successful people who got caught up in the dynamics of the situation. They were frozen in their own beliefs about what was happening.

Ironically, the board thought that firing the CEO was courageous. They would admit their mistake, face the consequences, and move on. Actually, this plan wasn't courageous. They were about to avoid some very hard work that would have them confront themselves, not just the CEO.

Meanwhile, the CEO was ready to quit. He felt stifled by the "stuck in the mud" board that was handcuffed to the past. After three months, he had decided the organization was hopeless. The board went from seeing a light at the end of a tunnel to feeling run over by a train. The CEO thought he had the opportunity to run full throttle but later realized the infrastructure couldn't take it.

The ease with which people get dug in to a position can be startling. Once in a camp, humans have a powerful tendency to see incoming information through the lens of self-confirming data. A well-known phenomenon, it leads even smart people to interpret new information in such a way that it does not challenge their *a priori* beliefs.

Telescopes and Microscopes

The board and chief executive of this organization did come to a much better understanding. They bravely sat down and talked through the issues, rumors, and ill feelings. They had to admit to falling prey to manipulation, which they admitted was embarrassing. We managed to keep things quiet, and this group continued to work together for the next six years.

At the time I got involved, the situation was what we in the South call a "hot mess." I like these messes. I spent a great deal of my residency at the Medical College of Georgia/Veterans Administration Consortium in Augusta, Georgia, working in emergency and high-stakes situations. I found a steady diet of routine corporate matters, frankly, boring. Crisis, on the other hand, is interesting. A board and chief executive officer who are battling each other is a crisis that must be addressed. The stakes are too high to avoid looking for the root of the problem.

I find that crises like those in the boardroom have something in common with the medical and psychiatric emergencies I encountered in my past: the tendency to use the wrong tool for the situation. A microscope is great for magnifying small things, but it tells you little about the shape of the organism within which the element resides. On the other hand, a telescope allows you to see a broader view from a distance, but it is unnecessary when you are looking at minute elements that are within reach. Each is valuable in its own way.

As is common, the client with the conflict between the board and CEO hired me and then offered suggestions about how to proceed. These were actually thinly veiled commands. I let them know that since I was the consultant, I would determine the method that would best achieve their desired result. They were handing me a microscope and telling me that the object of study was to be the CEO. I knew this was a more complicated problem, so I rejected their recommendation. When the stakes are high and people feel responsible for making them so, even leaders who usually perform very well can make mistakes such as assuming the accuracy of what they are told. Once we assume that we have the facts, it is not easy to go back and ask, how do I know that?

I began speaking with the executive committee of the board and the CEO. It didn't take long to see what was happening. As soon as people had privacy to talk, I found out that two board members were actively undermining the new leader. No one had bothered to confirm what they were told. After all, they were hearing it from trusted colleagues. Not only were they depending on a microscope, but they weren't even using it themselves.

If the strategists are using telescopes, then the primary tool of technical experts and operators is a microscope. Leaders need to know which to use, and when. Too many are stuck using, and overusing, their preferred tool, whether it is grapevine scoop, analysis, sales report, or economic forecast.

When I was learning to drive, I was very lucky to be in a public school system that had driver's education. We had simulators that allowed us to practice without risking life and limb. Our teachers received real-time feedback about how we did. Brake too late? Fail to signal? Do a sort-of stop at the traffic light? They knew right away. They could tell if your eyes were on your dashboard too long or if they rarely were. They taught us to move our eyes, looking out and around, and to check our speed regularly.

Great leaders don't get stuck in a point of view, on particular methodology, or with a single instrument. No matter how well something has served in the past, it may be wrong for what is in front of us now. It may be wildly inappropriate for the future. Yet, it takes courage to look at oneself and ask, What do I need to change about myself, my methods, the tools I am using?" The people who can do this most easily have developed their courage and learned that the rewards of courage are far greater than those they can achieve by avoidance.

The Irreplaceable You

When the founders of The Home Depot, a company near and dear to my heart, decided it was time to step aside in favor of a professional corporate leader, they hired Robert Nardelli. Arthur Blank and Bernie Marcus, two well-known and beloved men in my adopted hometown of Atlanta, started The Home Depot with little more than an idea, a dream.

You can look online and find some of the old commercials for The Home Depot. Watch a few of these old ads as if you don't know that this company now has a market capitalization of more than $165 billion. Would you have invested in this company? In the 1990s, The Home Depot's price/earnings ratio routinely ran high, signaling greater risk. They were scrappy, and the stores were, and still are, more like warehouses than like retail spaces. In full disclosure, I love The Home Depot.

In the beginning, the founders who are most associated with the company—Bernie Marcus and Arthur Blank—used the power of their enthusiasm to motivate the employees. They also had the brilliant idea to have tradesmen working in the stores. You could walk in with a part that had fallen off your dishwasher or faucet, hold it out, and ask, "Can you tell me what this is, where to get a new one, and how to install it?" They would do it. Happily. My husband and I have been known to measure home improvement projects in both dollars and number of trips to The Home Depot. This has far more to do with our limited skills than any bad advice we might have received.

The focus on customer service was extraordinary. The company grew and grew. People who started out in frontline jobs now hold some of the most elevated positions in the company. Ann-Marie Campbell started her career as a cashier and now runs all the retail stores for the United States—the job once occupied by Frank Blake's successor, Marvin Ellison. Campbell is on the board of Potbelly Sandwich Company and was on the board of Barnes & Noble. The way Campbell leads is a testament not only to her character but also to the legacy of Marcus and Blank.

When The Home Depot grew to the point that it needed a bit more internal focus, on matters such as inventory, supply chain, purchasing, and so forth, the board brought in Nardelli, who had been in the running for CEO of GE. The next few years were not great for The Home Depot in terms of customer service and the motivation and engagement of employees. Nardelli changed the company in some ways that it needed to change and in some ways that were disastrous. He knew the result he wanted, but he didn't understand how to get it. He didn't understand that The Home Depot's unique culture drove the customer experience. Finally, after a well-known falling out with the board, he left the company. The publicity surrounding his compensation—during his tenure and especially upon his unceremonious departure—was extraordinary. Shareholders were furious, people in Atlanta were incensed, and the money shows had lots to talk about.

In the midst of this brouhaha, Frank Blake took over as CEO, and the company's employees were thrilled. The actions he took were as well received as Nardelli's were rejected. He closed the executive dining room, and soon the GE alums who had followed Nardelli to The Home Depot began to depart. Not all of them—Frank Blake had also been at GE—but he was a very different sort of person. He looked at the company holistically and from the outside in, as well as from the inside out.

I have observed that great leaders do not stare at spreadsheets and then make big decisions. Nor do they walk around talking to people as their primary source of information. They use multiple methods and multiple sources of data. The primary tool they use is their own ability to learn in various ways.

Frank Blake and Ann-Marie Campbell are examples of leaders who look at the mosaic, not just the tiles or just the grout or only at a piece of the picture or only where it is located. They look at the entirety and use their judgment to decide what information to weigh most heavily, and when.

Perhaps the most important thing that they exemplify is the value of knowing who you are and having the courage to stay true to yourself. Sincere focus on the best interests of the company, customers, and employees and the well-being of others is evidenced in what they do at work, certainly. It goes well beyond that.

Courage in the Breach

Just after Frank Blake announced that he would be retiring and the board named Craig Menear to succeed him, The Home Depot experienced a major breach of its IT system. Blake could have said to Menear, "Well, what a shame for you to have this happen so soon, good luck." He didn't do that.

Instead, his behavior provides a model:

1. Admit the problem.
2. Apologize to those impacted.
3. Support those who will be in the crosshairs.
4. Organize a response and stay close to it.
5. Show that you take responsibility by what you do, not just by saying you are doing so.

When data breaches occur, customers want to know one thing: What does it mean for me? The answer came swiftly. In a *Fortune* article, writer

Jennifer Reingold said it beautifully, "Within a few hours of that initial phone call, the company apologized to its customers in a statement—mercifully free of mealy-mouthed corporate jargon—on its website and assured them that they would not be liable for any fraudulent charges."[2] A few days later, Frank Blake sent out a personal message apologizing for the breach.

If we scan the history of organizations, it is easy to see how quickly things go terribly wrong when we sidestep, hide, or fool ourselves. Richard Feynman was speaking of very different technology when he made this remark, but his comments are valid: "Reality must take precedence over public relations."

It's easy for us to read Feynman's comment and agree. It's much harder to act in the way we think best when we are in the midst of a crisis, or what feels like one.

The examples from political life are numerous and well known. John Edwards and Anthony Weiner come to mind. Both denied what they were accused of—creating elaborate lies to cover up. In the end, the cover-ups made them look worse than the thing they were trying to hide. Attempts to prevent a crisis once a mistake has been made can cause things to go from bad to worse. Another way things go wrong is when leaders minimize the crisis, either to others or to themselves.

First, Know You Are in a Crisis. Second, Act Like You Know

When an oil rig in the Gulf of Mexico exploded and led to death, catastrophic leaking of oil, and significant environmental and economic damage, we watched in horror. British Petroleum, led at the time by Tony Hayward, didn't respond the way we would hope. The company was overconfident in its ability to stop the leak, vastly underestimated how long it would take, and showed little sympathy for the residents of the coast who would, surely, be impacted.

Tony Hayward didn't act like he recognized the crisis. Contrast this attitude with the behavior of Frank Blake. Blake knew the company had a crisis on its hands and that it went far beyond a technical matter. Customers would be worried and wonder about the ability of The Home Depot to keep their information safe. Employees would face customers who would have questions, concerns and, perhaps, accusations. The IT team would wonder what they missed, perhaps be worried for their jobs, and certainly be concerned about their reputation, both collective and individual. Blake supported the IT team, expressing confidence in their ability to not only solve the current issue but also improve the company's systems for the long haul. He wondered what he had done, or not done, that contributed. In short, he looked for cause, sought remediation and improvement, and did not look for whom to blame.

Ignorance Is Not Bliss

It seems obvious that leaders will recognize when they are in a crisis, or when one is looming. They don't always. The ability to recognize impending threats consistently, over a long period of time, is nearly superhuman. Our cognitive and perceptual abilities are influenced by environment—both external (family, roles, region, culture, etc.) and internal (neurochemicals, personal style, and habits). We can vastly increase the likelihood of information, cues, clues, and advice from getting through to us. We can also close our eyes and minds.

The Greatest Vulnerability Is Not from Lack of Information, But from Smugness

Ask anyone what they remember about Tony Hayward. I'll bet they'll say, "I want my life back." Whatever he did before the oil spill and whatever he said after that, this is what we remember. That is a sad legacy. One that he most surely did not create intentionally. Fear and anxiety can make us blind to what we might otherwise recognize. Panic can lead us to do things that we realize later are foolish—but it can also fuel acts of great courage. Emotional energy is a powerful thing. It fuels behavior.

Anxiety-Fueled Crisis

The transition from one chief executive officer to another is a high-stakes situation. The emotion of the outgoing CEO can have a powerful impact on both the process and the outcome. In the most difficult situations, the outgoing CEO leaves a trail of damaged relationships and, rather than a positive legacy, a sense of relief that he is finally gone.

Most chief executives work their way to the job through a series of roles with increasing responsibility, expanding their networks, knowledge, and influence. They aren't usually in a hurry to move out of the role, even when doing so may be the best thing. It is understandable that this would be a difficult change for an individual, and that is precisely why they should not be left to figure out the transition process on their own.

Some CEOs stay at the party too long. They hang on, don't prepare an internal successor, or form relationships with a possible external successor. In the most challenging cases, they are adversarial with the board on the topic and actively, though perhaps unconsciously, undermine possible successors.

Recalcitrant CEOs don't seem to understand that it isn't just their legacy they are playing with. A contentious succession process tarnishes more than the reputation of a CEO who is hanging on for dear life. It also tarnishes the company.

How does this happen? Multiple ways.

First, the struggles in the boardroom have a way of leaking out. Not necessarily because a director is inappropriately sharing what is going on. Rather, boards have observers. Shareholders, employees, competitors, analysts, commentators, and the financial press are all observers. The CEO will be asked questions, and the answers can reveal more than she intends.

A CEO who is in conflict with her board is distracted. The relationship between the board and CEO will show signs of strain. The tension between Michael Eisner and the Disney board, Carly Fiorina and the board of Hewlett-Packard, and Bob Nardelli and The Home Depot board are unfortunate public examples.

As distracting as this conflict may be, it is far better than the situation in which a weak board allows itself to be pushed around by a bully CEO. Yet, the boardroom is a place occupied by human beings.

Long before a rift is noticeable to outsiders, a CEO's decisions will be influenced by the uncertainty and fear she feels at having her future—including her date of departure—determined by someone else. Once others begin to notice that the CEO's actions seem influenced by a need to hold on to a position, the suspicions grow like wildfire.

Worry about an impending event of unknown timing leads to a distorted view of information, people, and risks. Eventually, the focus goes to the board. What are they doing or not doing? How did they let this happen?

Just as an individual's behavior can be driven by anxiety, so can it be driven by a desire to keep the anxiety at bay. Others may tiptoe around it for fear of igniting conflict. A board without a process to rely upon can easily kick the can down the road for years, as long as the sitting CEO wants to stay and there is no obvious reason to press the issue.

This is just as negligent as failing to have financial audits. Arranging for CEO succession is a vital role of the board. Yet, many think of CEO succession as an event, and one to be dreaded. This is an ostrich plan, and the problem with those is that you don't see the truck coming right at you.

Fortunately, many companies successfully go through changes at the CEO level with either absent or weak succession processes. I've seen many, and even though we make it work, I still long for my clients to adopt a more systematic process that will prevent crises in the future. Why don't they? Because having come through a crisis, they breathe a sigh of relief. They are loath to stay on the topic that just caused them such agony. Usually, they believe that the issue won't come up again for a long time, which is likely true. Furthermore, it feels wrong to talk to a newly appointed CEO about succession.

There is one reason that trumps all the others. Succession planning is a behavioral process. It relies on what people do. No fancy automated process can replace the attention and judgment of the people who are involved. The following continuum (see Figure 2.1) shows where CEO succession falls between an automated process and one that relies on human action.

The reason I place the X slightly to the right of the far end is that there is some information that can and should feed into a process such as leadership succession, without additional effort. These are the objective measures such as revenue, margin, sales, rate of growth, market share, and so forth that are, or should be, known for a given senior executive.

The other aspects of the majority of successions are behavioral, attitudinal, or based on capacity. Attention must be given to the way the person achieves what she does. These are, necessarily, descriptive, and most are qualitative, but that does not mean they are irrelevant.

When considering a process that is more or less behavioral and gauging the amount of anxiety that is provoked by the issue, consider the results in the following matrix (see Figure 2.2).

My experience tells me that people spend far too much time in the lower right quadrant. A leader who does not address the high-risk but low-frequency or low-probability events will eventually be caught in a damaging situation. CEO succession is one such example. Others include failure of critical systems, such as the failure, in summer 2016, of the Delta Airlines computer system, which left thousands of customers stranded when the company was forced to cancel or delay more than 4,000 flights. Very high risk and very low probability, but still disastrous. Unfortunately, Delta

Figure 2.1 *Behavior—Automated*

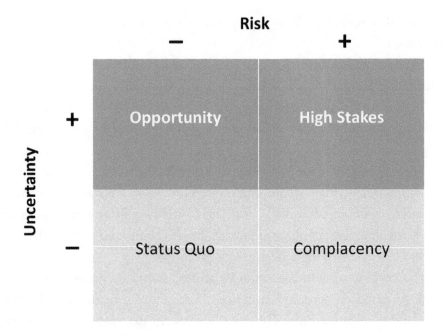

Figure 2.2 *High-Stakes Leadership*

experienced a similar failure in 2017, once again stranding thousands of its customers.

Avoidance-Fueled Crisis

The very first CEO succession process I was involved with, decades ago, had a particular aspect to it that I have thought about many times. The organization was in bad financial shape, with revenue declining in all but one aspect of the business. The CEO ruled with an iron fist and the board had been too trusting. The upside was the organization had a very good reputation, a long and storied history, and thousands of customers ready to continue doing business. The struggle was in attracting new customers. It's easy to see what would eventually happen.

The leading candidate—in my opinion, and in the opinion of my colleague, Dr. Joe McGill—asked to see the financial reports for the previous three years. After reviewing them, he pulled out of the running for the job.

He said he couldn't take on the job because the measures required for the long-term health of the company were too draconian for his taste. He said, "I'm not the guy to do that."

Now the board had a real dilemma: not only did one of three most promising candidates leave the race, but he also raised an issue that the board hadn't seen in the way this candidate did. While they did not ignore the problem, neither did they respond with the vigor they should have. They let it slide.

The board did understand that they needed a visionary leader, someone with a fine, strategic mind and the energy to implement bold new ideas. They found such a person and breathed a temporary sigh of relief. A few short months later, the chairman of the board was on the phone telling me about the misdeeds of the new CEO. He was developing new ideas to grow the company and talking to people in the industry—outside of the four walls of his office. He was brash, moved too fast, and hadn't kept the board in the loop.

Further fueling the discord between the board and CEO was the company's financial situation. The new CEO dug into the financials soon after taking the role and found what his former competitor had discovered: a disaster was looming. The financial path the company was on gave the new CEO pause and, yes, made him anxious. His already impatient nature became more pronounced once he had the inside view.

The board felt that the new CEO had an attitude of superiority, and the CEO wondered how the board had let this bad financial situation happen. They did what people often do—blame one another rather than look for causes and solutions. It was a full-on mess, even without the complication of the inappropriate relationship of the board chairman and a senior staff person.

Solution in Plain Sight

Fortunately, the solution lay in plain sight. This group needed to get on the same page, and quickly. The executive committee of the board agreed to take on the issue(s) and to put a boundary around their work until they had something to share with the rest of the board other than "this is a mess." They asked for help and listened to my summary of the situation. First, the organization had big problems that had gone unaddressed in the past. Second, the previous CEO had been less than candid and had muzzled some of the senior staff. Third, the board had not done a great job of oversight. Fourth, the new CEO did not understand what sort of relationship the board, and particularly the chairman, expected. Neither had he made a good attempt to find out.

Finally, their choice now was to either work to make it better or continue on the current path, which was taking them over the cliff.

When You Put It That Way

The chairman, upon hearing my review said, "Well, that's embarrassing. We've been acting like children in a schoolyard fight." To which I replied, "Yes, but you can change it now. Let's understand the causes of what has happened and fix them. Don't beat yourself up and don't beat up your colleagues; let's move on."

If I had not seen it myself, I would think that the following is an utter fabrication. The group got together, listened to what I had to say, and spontaneously apologized to one another. They were shaken and embarrassed. Once they had a few minutes of mea culpa, I suggested we talk about what was next. The rest of the day, we talked about the future, how to best improve the organization, and how they needed to work together to make it happen. Their relationships were never the same. Even when someone slid back into their old ways, there were others to remind them of what that had created in the past and of their commitments to one another and the company.

The people in this story are all smart, successful, experienced, and well-meaning individuals. They created a crisis because they avoided situations that they should have elevated to near-crisis levels, but didn't. The dismal outlook and poor financial results should have generated some heated dialogue and new directions. It didn't. The long-serving, controlling CEO should have been dealt with in strong and clear terms. He wasn't. The board treated their meetings as part work, but mostly as vacation on the company's dime; members should have looked at themselves in an unfogged mirror. They didn't. Any one of these issues could have been raised to a level of significance that it deserved, despite protests that would have surely been leveled.

The drive to reduce tension and anxiety is a powerful one. We humans will do things to reduce fear—our own and others—even when doing so makes the future worse. Leaders need to have the nerve to elevate important matters to a high level and create energy and urgency around them. Otherwise, the issues we avoid become the kindling for a forest fire.

Intentional Crisis

Leaders need to create energy, get people focused, and inspire the behaviors needed to reach a goal. I once worked with a surgeon who could get the most sluggish person to move with great speed, in the right direction, simply by using his voice in a very directed way. He issued loud, clear instructions, made lots of eye contact, and was utterly unambiguous. I recall his instructing someone to get him coffee. He said, "Cream and four sugars." She replied, "That's a lot of sugar." "You can't start a bonfire without a pile of kindling," he yelled. Needless to say, almost everyone who worked around him was afraid of him. He was a very good surgeon, his patients loved him, and he was called into the most challenging cases—even those that didn't require a surgeon. He commanded attention, which he used to get all eyes on the patient and what needed to be done.

The style of this surgeon—and he is by no means unique in the profession—is to get things going in the right direction quickly. This is a quality that leaders can emulate: impatience.

Courageous Impatience

Impatience with an evolutionary approach to societal wrongs is often decried. Indeed, Branch Rickey, the Hall of Fame baseball player and manager, said,

> They call you an extremist if you want integration now—which is the only morally defensible position. To advise moderation is like going to a stickup man and saying to him: 'Don't use a gun. That's violent. Why not be a pickpocket instead?' A moderate is a moral pickpocket.

Rickey was, of course, the man who brought Jackie Robinson to the Brooklyn Dodgers. He did so for two reasons: (1) he believed that different and wrong treatment of nonwhites was morally wrong, and (2) he believed that it was foolish to look for baseball talent only among Caucasians.

A simple recounting of Branch Rickey's act to bring Jackie Robinson to the Dodgers risks making both men seem too simple. Rickey had been troubled by segregation and violence against blacks for years, though he had done little about it. Against the backdrop of Jim Crow, the Supreme Court's Dred Scott decision, and institutionalized racism, his desire to pick the spot where he could make an impact is understandable.

Robinson grew up with the realities of racism but used his considerable talents to establish a good reputation which, in turn, gave him credibility and stature in refusing ill treatment. Opposing unfair treatment did not always result in the outcome he sought, such as when he was on a military bus and refused to move to the back. Later, he would be subjected to court-martial on charges that would be reduced to insubordination.

Robinson was expected to be an exemplary man in every way—not under normal circumstances, but in the face of open opposition to him playing on the Dodgers team. In the face of open hostility, bigotry, name calling, and opposition at every turn, he had to summon superhuman control to keep his anger in check. On this, he and Rickey agreed from the start. Perhaps Rickey did not know that Jackie Robison had a lot of practice dealing with unfairness while keeping his head about him. This combination of extraordinary talent and self-control was pivotal.

Branch Rickey knew that it would take bold action to change the course of history for baseball. He was impatient but still looked for an opportunity, and most especially for the person he felt could withstand the hostility that would surely come his way. Rickey knew the potential firestorm that bringing Robinson onto the team would cause and knew that it could even prove dangerous.

We celebrate Jackie Robinson for his athletic gifts, and as a role model, trail blazer, and person of admirable and courageous character. We should. He is the only baseball star honored by having every player wear his number, forty-two, each year on April 15—the date he first played in the major leagues. This not only honors Robinson but allows every person watching any game on that day to learn about him and be reminded that the institution of baseball was once as segregated as the rest of our country. The honor is no more than deserved. Jackie Robinson was Rookie of the Year, was an All-Star every year from 1949 to 1954, played in the World Series six times, and is in the Hall of Fame.

Branch Rickey should also be appreciated for the role he played in bringing the talents of Robinson to the major leagues. He planned it, used judgment, showed courage, and found a man whose own courage was more than sufficient to make it work.

Notes

1. John Bierman, *Righteous Gentile*. New York: Penguin (1996).
2. Jennifer Reingold, "How Home Depot CEO Frank Blake Kept His Legacy From Being Hacked," October 29, 2014, accessed February 15, 2017, http://fortune.com/2014/10/29/home-depot-cybersecurity-reputation-frank-blake/.

CHAPTER 3

Culture

Culture describes the pattern of shared assumptions and behaviors that a group adopts, usually over time and often without intention. Common behaviors in a culture at one point in time may make sense in terms of achieving the goals of a group. In companies, culture can be like an invisible electric fence. You can't see it, but you know where it is when you feel the shock.

Wall Street Blues

My first day at Merrill Lynch, after passing the dreaded Series 7 exam and spending weeks in New York for training, I was sitting in my cube when I noticed that the men in the office gathered in the lobby. At exactly 11:45 a.m., they all walked out of the building together. To lunch, of course, but to my new-broker eyes, it looked like they were going to a meeting. The next day? Same thing.

When I asked a female colleague about it, she said, "Yeah, they do that every day." I asked if they ever invited their female colleagues (there were three of us), and she said they never did. I went to lunch by myself a couple times, with a female colleague often, and sometimes with a couple of the women who worked in support roles. Then I got a talking to. "Don't hang out with the secretaries," I was told.

That's culture. Violate the norms and you'll find out where the fence is. Ask about the fence, and most people won't be able to tell you much. Some could tell you, but in a hostile culture, they'd rather watch you walk into it.

In hindsight, I realized that every time we hired a new broker, it was a high-stakes situation, especially for them. There was hazing, of sorts, to go along with the stress of having to pass the Series 7 exam (pass it or be fired). Especially for women, the office was a very inhospitable place, as evidenced by multiple successful lawsuits against the firm. Support staff were reshuffled, and someone would be stuck with the new kid.

The operations head would be annoyed because the new broker would inevitably make many mistakes with orders to trade. Our manager's assistant gave up information only under duress, never proactively. The office manager was present but uninvolved. Even people who told filthy jokes in his presence got no rebuke. This is how a bad culture is sustained—by looking the other way.

Because most brokers wash out in the first two years, no one tried very hard to help a new person. The saying "churn 'em and burn 'em" was not just about getting clients to generate commissions; it could have just as easily pertained to the high failure rate of brokers. When a corporate culture is focused on individual behavior, as this one was, managers don't look at things systemically. If talent retention is low everywhere, no one thinks much about it.

I thought a lot about it, however. The environment made me profoundly unhappy. Even in a good month, when I earned more money than ever, I was miserable. So, I quit. I daresay not a single person I worked with thought the cause of my leaving was anything other than my being ill suited for the job. Even me.

Years later, when I was sitting on a stage with Alan Weiss—the man who would later become my mentor—he asked me about my background. I talked about what I had done since leaving the financial industry. He guided me through the conversation with great questions that helped me see what I had accomplished. At the end, he said, "And Merrill Lynch doesn't have you."

During the time I worked at Merrill Lynch, and especially when I decided to leave, my focus was on my future. What did I really want to do, and how was I going to get there? Only in hindsight did it occur to me that the culture was a terrible fit for me, and only when Alan Weiss pointed out that they lost my talent did I see the bigger picture. If an organization hires people different from those they historically brought on board but the context doesn't change, the benefits will be few.

Cultural Overhaul

A chairman of the board was receiving anonymous letters about the chief executive officer. In the letters, the CEO was accused of being a tyrant, behaving in an abusive manner toward employees, having an affair with a subordinate, and threatening people who did not agree with him. The chairman was very concerned, but also surprised. He asked the human resources leader about the accusations and was assured that they were true. The situation, as described in the letters, she said, was indeed what was happening.

The chairman, a man of great experience and mature judgment, wondered if the human resources leader had an ax to grind. He also knew that he couldn't dismiss the allegations, even if he was inclined to believe they were exaggerated. The chairman and I spoke, and we agreed that I should look into things further.

What I found was nearly as bad as the letters suggested. Everything was true, except the claim of the affair, which was untrue. There was more, however, that even the letter writer(s) had missed. Now, we had a bigger problem: a CEO who was creating risk and people in the organization who were willing to make damning claims about him, though some of the claims were not well founded.

The chairman quickly looped in the rest of the board and gained their agreement to remove the CEO. Problem solved, right? No. Removing one person does not solve a systemic issue.

Among the accusations in the anonymous letters were accusations about the board. These were all either untrue or reflected the writer's lack of understanding about the role of a board. That is, the writer assumed the board should manage the organization. This made me suspicious that a few things might be true. First, was the writer an aggrieved person who was going to be satisfied that the former leader had been removed? Second, was there a group of angry, disgruntled employees who might be on the lookout for the next thing to be angry about? Third, if the grievances were not resolved, what move might an individual or group make next?

This is what began to happen right away: rumors about the new CEO and his lack of concern for employees were spreading. The stories about how lousy the board had been persisted. Every decision, every communication, every action—or inaction—was scrutinized through the most cynical lens you can imagine. The place was, in a word, rotten. It was a full-on crisis.

So, what did the new CEO do?

- Addressed the employees and apologized for the poor environment.
- Gave everyone a pass for past bad behavior. He admitted that the previous leader had created problems.
- Promised a new day and provided a plan for how that would work.
- Fired senior executives who were negative and cynical.
- Improved professional development.

These were all important, but by far the most significant actions that led to dramatic change were these two specific things: first, when someone demonstrated that he was hell-bent on remaining angry and embittered, he was removed. This happened only when the employee's observable behavior indicated an attitude that was unsuitable. Examples included repeating negative and untrue stories, sharing erroneous assumptions and accusations, and offering cynical interpretations, and those who sought allies in the war against the new CEO were a special focus.

Second, those who had grievances but brought them forward in a constructive manner were promoted. The message? Complain in a way that allows us to use your input to become better and we'll reward you. It took more than a year to accomplish the change, but it happened.

The new CEO knew this was a high-stakes situation. He was either going to change the culture or be a victim of it.

Merging Cultures

Though culture plays a role in an organization's ability to execute its strategy, the issue comes into stark relief in mergers and acquisitions. Organizational culture is commonly believed to be so difficult that some leaders even get off the hook when they report that a deal didn't work out due to "culture clashes."

In the late 1990s, a young, small, and highly successful company in the household products industry wanted to dramatically increase shareholder value in a different way. It merged with a larger, much older company that had brands in the same industry. The companies were Reckitt & Colman— makers of Lysol—and Benckiser, whose best-known product was Jet Dry. The chief operating officer of Benckiser, Bart Becht, became chief executive officer of the newly formed Reckitt Benckiser and set about bringing together these two global companies.

To say that Reckitt & Colman and Benckiser were different is a grand understatement. Reckitt & Colman was started in 1814. When I was in the company's offices in Windsor, England, one day, I realized looking out a window that it was located next to Windsor Castle. The good news? Reckitt had stability. The bad news? Same thing. The company had good products and brand equity, but slow growth. It was as if the castle next door had a leaky moat that was leaking tradition and reluctance to modernize right into the offices of Reckitt & Colman.

Benckiser, a much younger company, was known for being agile and extremely disciplined. The people at Benckiser were the most relentlessly focused I had seen since leaving my hometown, where our local heroes were astronauts and test pilots.

Bart Becht did what I now advise all my clients do when acquiring or merging. First, if your deal is a merger, don't let that make you equivocal. When named chief executive officer of the newly formed company, Becht could have vacillated or been conciliatory, concerned about upsetting a few apple carts. Had he done that, he would have been moved by the sheer gravitational pull of the Reckitt & Colman culture and the values and beliefs underlying it. Instead, he moved people—both emotionally and literally—and the culture he intended to build quickly emerged.

Later, when Reckitt Benckiser acquired Boots Healthcare, I helped the company with key decisions. This time, I knew exactly where Becht was headed and how laser focused he was on creating shareholder value. I didn't need to be reminded about the culture or the type of people they were looking for, so clear, simple, and powerful were both the vision and the means to get there.

The culture was seen as a driving force, and people were selected according to how good they were *and* how well they fit the culture that Becht and his team were creating. Once selected, they were expected to perform, and were given the latitude to do so. Benckiser had many very young people in management positions. Top managers sent junior people to countries where they had never been and told them to get the business going. They succeeded with astonishing frequency. Why? Leaders chose them on the basis of clear criteria tied directly to the strategic objectives, including how well they fit into the company's "go get 'em" culture.

I recall Amy, a rising star in the company, entering the room for our meeting rumpled and rattled from having spent the night in her office, unable to go home because of a hurricane. She looked too young to have a job at all, never mind a big role. Amy told me about being sent to a country in Eastern Europe to get things going. Those were her instructions. She did exactly that. She offered a lesson in focus, discipline, decisiveness, and perseverance. Her leaders demonstrated confidence in her and proved it by giving her the role and letting her figure out how to do it. Amy represents the type of person the company often sent to undeveloped markets. The leaders didn't second-guess their decisions. Had they been equivocal, the confidence of those they selected, like Amy, would have been undermined.

The investment that Bart Becht made in choosing the best people was not small. His radical focus on getting people who fit the culture was seen, by some, as fierce. It paid off. The newly merged company's share price doubled in two years.

Behavior Predicts Attitudes

Leaders often talk about the need to change the attitudes of people in their organization. Usually, they are looking for their people to have a sense of ownership over what they are doing, and to be enthusiastic, open minded, and action oriented. The first problem is that we can't see attitudes, only behavior. The second problem is that people are not very skilled at reporting attitudes directly—that is, in response to direct questions. This makes intervening at the level of attitudes very challenging, time consuming, fraught with error, and distracting.

A more accurate and reliable way to think about attitudes is by considering the way they are shaped by experience. Most people, most of the time, espouse attitudes that are consistent with their experience, environment, and their behavior. For example, when people live in an area where their neighbors routinely recycle, they are more likely to do so themselves and more likely to say that they believe in the value of recycling.

Cleaning Up a Mess

In a warehouse, where I was consulting for the general manager, most of the people cleaned up after themselves in the break room. This courtesy was part of the way they did things; but that wasn't true when this manager first arrived. He told me these were the messiest people he'd ever seen, and it drove him crazy. He asked me, "How do I get them to care?" He was trying to figure out how to intervene at the level of attitude.

Rather than tackle it that way, I suggested a different approach. I asked the general manager to sit with people who did a good job of cleaning up after themselves. At the end of the mealtime, he made sure his own area was spotless. When a group that was notoriously messy asked him to sit with them, he said, "Of course, but I want us to all clean up our space together before we leave, okay?"

What was this man doing? He was changing the norms, not by scolding or lecturing but by his own behavior and by giving the reward of his company to employees who followed his lead.

Now, you are thinking that this is a pretty insignificant example. It is. But it makes several points. First, it is an example of "social proof," a psychological phenomenon investigated and beautifully described by Dr. Robert Cialdini.[1] Social proof is the influence that the behavior of some have on the behavior of others. People look to what others are doing if they are unsure what to do themselves. Even when we think we are sure, we are influenced by the behavior of those around us; this is true of all humans, whether they see the behavior or just hear about it.

Second, the break room example illustrates the power of a leader's behavior. Ralph, the general manager in my example, was a very tidy person. If he hadn't been, he would have been a poor choice to be part of the intervention we designed. He was well known for being a "neat freak," but he wasn't so well known for being a good lunch companion. As he got to know more people, and they him, he had more influence and didn't need to rail against the "slobs."

Did everyone fall in line? No, of course not. Remember, I said people are more likely to do what those around them do, but not everyone will follow. Exceptions do not disprove principles like the power of social proof. Because Ralph was running a warehouse, where there is danger of falling inventory, forklift accidents, truck accidents, loading accidents, and so on, order and tidiness is of high value. Injuries and deaths on the job are not only emotionally painful, they are damaging all the way around. Losses from damaged inventory in the warehouse that Ralph was responsible for totaled $8,000 a month when we first met. See, the tidiness in the break room wasn't an isolated situation. We got the inventory losses down too, by the way.

What if you need innovation? Can the same ideas of social proof and leader behavior be applied? Yes.

The Transformer

In 2015, when Rachel Moore took over as chief executive officer for the Los Angeles Music Center—the home of the Los Angeles Philharmonic, Opera, Center Theatre Group, and Los Angeles Master Chorale—the organization was struggling with issues similar to those faced by many arts organizations. Fortunately, Moore had just left her leadership post at the American Ballet Theatre in New York City, where she had been successful in a similar circumstance. Moore believes firmly that "art transforms lives." When she says it, you become a believer.

The staff at the Los Angeles Music Center had been through downsizing and disappointing fund-raising and was, understandably, nervous about what this new leader would do. They were, quite rightly, fearful that more cuts were coming. Moore knew that simply telling the staff that it was a new day wouldn't get them anywhere. Mindful that her biggest mistakes as a leader had been in "not listening," she wasn't about to make that mistake again.

Right away, Moore began talking with people in the community and the people who worked at the Music Center. And not just her direct reports—everyone. She learned about how the place worked, what ideas people had to make it better, and how people were feeling about the future. This gave her both information and insight about what was important, and to whom. While she observed attitudes, she didn't assume that they were fixed for all time. She believed that giving people a sense of direction and underlining why that course is important is the job of a leader, not telling them how to take every step to get there. In her view, a leader must provide the tools for achievement rather than being a gatekeeper of ideas or a barrier to be crossed. These are things that change attitudes about work and improve the energy level, but not by saying it—by doing it.

In her first year, the staff came up with an idea they called "Sleepless: The Music Center After Hours," a program targeted at people who do not typically come to events at the Music Center. "Sleepless" was a late-night party with artists of various types, cocktails, food, and lots of beanbag chairs into which participants could collapse if they chose. DJs, video displays, and opportunities to go behind the scenes created an experience at the Dorothy Chandler Pavilion unlike anything that been seen there before. The events sold out immediately. The venue not only had an event unlike any it had held in the past, but it also had hundreds of people who attended talking about the experience. And those who missed the chance to buy a ticket were waiting eagerly for the next event's tickets to go on sale.

The staff at the Music Center had good reason to adopt an enthusiastic attitude. They had seen a new idea take off. This is how a leader can shape attitudes—by providing the opportunity for people to succeed, have autonomy over their work, and enjoy the results.

A leader who has the courage to let go and allow people the autonomy to do their jobs creates an attractive environment. Motivation and innovation grow where talented people have the latitude to create, experiment, and, yes, fail. When the stakes are high, leaders may seek more control, not less. This is a breeding ground for fear and resentment, not new ideas. Rachel Moore knows that turning the tide at the Music Center won't be accomplished by edict. Rather, it will come from unleashing creativity that, in turn, fuels motivation, leading to more innovation in a cycle that needs little meddling from the leader (see Figure 3.1). It needs a compass, not a checklist.

The staff at the Music Center should celebrate the success of their "Sleepless" events. Celebrating when a new idea comes to fruition is important, even when it does not produce such positive results. Why? Because celebrating and reminding people that they have the freedom and tools to invent, create, execute, and experiment fuels motivation and makes them want to do more. Quashing energy is one of the most damaging things a leader can do. Even when something doesn't turn out as well as we would like, the drive to do new things must be protected and celebrated.

A culture that breeds new ideas cannot celebrate only success. That leads people to hide failure, to be ashamed. An innovative culture is an environment in which *the work itself* is rewarding. When people, collectively, have the courage to take risks and learn from mistakes as well as celebrate success, they have an asset that should be nurtured and protected because you can't buy a replacement.

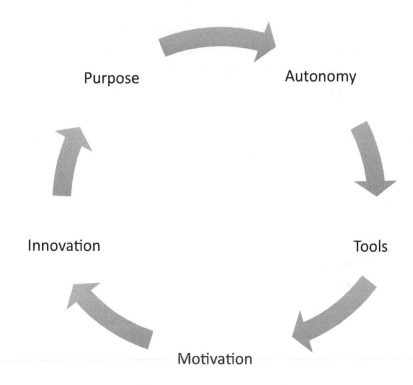

Figure 3.1 *Innovation Cycle*

Separated by a Common Language

I walked, bleary eyed, to the Border Force agent at the airport in Sydney one morning after the fifteen-and-a-half-hour flight from LAX. The agent asked, in a surprisingly happy voice, "How ya goin'?" Hmm . . . how ya goin' . . . does that mean where am I going? Seeing my confusion, he modified his question. "How are you?" asked the agent. Ah! That cleared it up.

The great thing about being in Australia and New Zealand with a North American accent is that they understand you. Why? Because they watch a lot of TV produced in the United States and Canada. The unlucky part is, it creates an unequal footing. They understood me very well, but I didn't understand them as easily. Seemed like they were doing all the work. Occasionally, I would run across someone who couldn't be bothered to help me understand what they were saying (it was rare), and I would be left confused. Most of you reading this have been in similar situations.

In business, when we are speaking the same language and dialect, we are fooled by something subtler than an accent. We are fooled by assumptions. Words and phrases sound the same but don't mean the same thing. Even from one business unit to another in the same company, expressions may be different. Here are just a few examples:

- Strategy
- Compliance
- Internal controls
- Timely reporting
- Transparency
- Succession planning
- Organizational culture
- Decisiveness
- Intelligence
- Buy–sell agreement
- Due diligence

People have a strong tendency to use what are known as *heuristics*. These are essentially frameworks or approaches, and they are helpful in simplifying our lives and the voluminous information that comes our way not just every day, but every hour. The issue with heuristics is not that they are wrong, rather that we use them when we shouldn't. And when shouldn't we? When they simplify to the point that important meaning is lost, when we are rushing into something and we don't want to be slowed down by more detail or analysis, or when we are making decisions under uncertain circumstances.

Overconfidence

Overconfidence plays a major role in decision making, and you probably surmise that it isn't helpful. It's tricky to deal with because it is a feeling, and most successful people don't care to admit that emotions play much of a role in serious decisions. When I was a resident, a professor put it in a way that I never forgot. He said, "Emotions are the fuel for behavior."

The phenomenon of overconfidence and its role in decision making is well documented by psychologists and explored further in experiments by behavioral economists. Daniel Kahneman and Amos Tversky's article "Judgment Under Uncertainty: Heuristics and Biases" is a classic, and is cited more than almost any other scholarly work in behavioral science.[2]

As with all phenomena of this type, we humans are largely unaware when we are experiencing something like overconfidence. Yet, the consequences of being overconfident can have consequences ranging from benign to disastrous. Here are a few examples:

- "Whatever happens, the U.S. Navy is not going to be caught napping": Frank Knox, U.S. Secretary of the Navy, three days before the attack on Pearl Harbor.
- "It would appear we have reached the limits of what it is possible to achieve with computer technology": computer scientist John von Neumann, 1949.
- By "next Christmas the iPod will be dead, finished, gone, kaput": Sir Alan Sugar, February 2005.
- "Ours has been the first, and doubtless to be the last, to visit this profitless locality": Lt. Joseph Ives, after visiting the Grand Canyon in 1861.
- "You want to have consistent and uniform muscle development across all of your muscles? It can't be done. It's just a fact of life. You just have to accept inconsistent muscle development as an unalterable condition of weight training": response to Arthur Jones, who solved the "unsolvable" problem by inventing Nautilus.

Why do these dramatic examples fail to influence us? Precisely because they are so dramatic. It's not so easy to extract the lessons and apply them to a situation that seems very different. Leaders often look to businesses like their own to make comparisons. That isn't enough. Dramatic growth doesn't come when we reassure ourselves that we are as good as the other guys.

This is why creating a culture of continuous learning is so vital. Principles must be applied in a variety of circumstances whose characteristics change. The application of principles, when done by rote, creates huge vulnerability. It swaps judgment for a habit and suspends the need for clear-eyed observation. Even habits or routines that have served us well need to be reexamined, preferably as a matter of health rather than crisis intervention.

This is not easy, as it involves letting go of beliefs that may have been dearly and long held. Even more challenging than the emotional tug to hold on, of which we are aware, is the unconscious nature of repeated behaviors and our need to justify our own behavior. Try the following quiz.

Provide a low and high answer for each question. Choose answers so that you have a 90 percent probability that the correct answer lies between the numbers you select (answers can be found at the end of the chapter).

	Low	High
1. John F. Kennedy's age at death	_____	_____
2. Height of Mt. Kilimanjaro	_____	_____
3. Number of countries in Africa	_____	_____
4. Area of California in square miles	_____	_____
5. Diameter of the earth (in miles)	_____	_____
6. Year of the *Challenger* shuttle disaster	_____	_____
7. Year the *Mona Lisa* was painted	_____	_____
8. Average weight of an Asian elephant	_____	_____
9. Distance from New York to Berlin (air miles)	_____	_____
10. Deepest point of the ocean (in feet)	_____	_____

Adapted from J. Edward Russo and Paul J. H. Schoemaker, *Winning Decisions: Getting It Right the First Time*, New York: Doubleday, 2001, 79–80. Used with permission.

Whether you are leading a company that requires a high level of compliance or innovation, you need people whose brains are engaged; people who have their eyes open, are curious and interested in learning; and people whose courage is cultivated by the environment so that problems aren't just solved but avoided and opportunities are seen and seized before the rest of the world sees them. A company's culture attracts either the right or the wrong people. Which kind of people does your company culture attract?

Answer key:

1. John F. Kennedy was 46 when he was assassinated.
2. Mt. Kilimanjaro rises 19,341 feet.
3. 54
4. 163,695
5. 7,917.5
6. 1986
7. 1507
8. Male – 12,000 lbs, Female – 6,000 lbs
9. 3,965
10. 36,200

Notes

1. Robert Cialdini, *Influence, Science and Practice.* 5th Edition. Pearson (2009), p. 99.
2. Amos Tversky and Daniel Kahneman, "Judgment Under Uncertainty: Heuristics and Biases," *Science* 185 (1974): 1124–1131.

CHAPTER 4

Strategic Courage

One of the more challenging aspects of working with clients on strategy is helping them let go. But, let go of what?

- Businesses that don't fit their strategy.
- Ideas that don't fit their strategy.
- People who are destructive to their goals.
- Habits—more often called *processes*—that don't work.

It is far easier to add goals, initiatives, task forces, and so forth than it is to let go of them when they don't work—especially for the person who added them in the first place. Once an executive has advocated for an action and implements it, she tends to hold on to it, no matter what. The evidence others see as reasons to make a change may be dismissed. Eventually, those who oppose what the executive wants to hold on to find themselves on the outs.

These situations aren't just caused by foolishness or ego, though sometimes that is the case. More often, they arise because people are acting like normal, everyday human beings. That is true of even the very analytical among you who are shaking your heads while reading this!

For example, leaders who advocate for an acquisition are less likely to sell it later, even if it performs poorly. While this scenario may be most likely, in truth, some leaders are great at dispassionately looking at their businesses to see what needs to go. Those leaders have a discipline about strategy. They don't just add, they edit. How do they do it?

- They evaluate all their businesses with the same rigor.
- They do not overstate the value of "goodwill."
- They look at capital allocation, which forces a holistic look.
- They manage their own emotions about loss.

A new leader can easily let go of what she didn't buy or build in the first place. After all, it wasn't her idea. A *Harvard Business Review* article reported that 50 percent of divestitures happen within two years of the appointment of a new CEO.[1] That's no accident.

What Stops Us from Stopping

Two phenomena that play a role in the inability of many leaders to abandon broken businesses, ideas, people, and processes are confirmation bias and sunk costs.

Confirmation bias leads us to take note of and give weight to information that confirms what we already believe. When confronted with disconfirming information, we sometimes dig in our heels. First, we doubt the evidence, then we discredit the method by which it came to light, and, finally, we attack the person who is giving us information that contradicts what we believe.

The notion of *sunk costs* says that having made investment X, we should keep investing so that we don't waste the original effort, time, and money. This leads many a person down an increasingly treacherous path. As Will Rogers once famously said, "If you find yourself in a hole, stop digging." This simple folk wisdom is worth remembering.

Bankers like to think of themselves as data-driven people. Even so, they tend to use less critical judgment once they have confidence in a client. They will make additional loans—even when a business isn't doing well—as long as their confidence in the business's leaders is intact. Notice that, despite the amount of data a bank has on a customer, human judgment plays a role in making decisions. Human judgment, we know, is influenced by emotion. One of the strongest such emotions is our need to avoid changing our minds. This leads to overweighting some information (I was right in the past) and underweighting other information (the circumstances have changed).

This leads people to hold onto relationships—both personal and business— that no longer work. Consultants continue to work with clients who are difficult, don't pay on time, and wreak havoc on schedules. Recently, a consultant told me that he spent ten months getting an agreement settled with a client—an agreement that would allow him to submit bids for work. Ridiculous! That isn't selling, and it sure isn't consulting. It's groveling, pure and simple. Holding out for months while clinging to shards of evidence is an example of the power of confirmation bias.

That Sinking Feeling

A CEO once told me, "I know I'm dealing with the issue of sunk costs when I have that sinking feeling in my stomach." He had just removed a chief operating officer after three years of trying to help him perform. The chief operating officer was mediocre, arrogant in his interactions with the board, and of questionable ethics. It was a relief to everyone when the CEO finally removed him. Only then did they discover just how much damage he caused. This is common, and many a leader learns the lesson in a similar way.

It reminded me of a chief executive officer for a Fortune 50 company who once said to me, "My most damaging mistakes have happened because I had a savior complex. I thought I could save people, businesses, products, relationships, anything. I didn't realize it until the evidence forced me to face it."

The false belief that we are helping—when we are actually enabling—is powerful. And it's especially hard to break when a leader's identity is that of "helper." Furthermore, once an investment of time, reputation, and emotion is made, we want to prove to ourselves, if not to others, that we were right to make the investment in the first place. Once we begin making decisions based on a need to prove that an earlier decision was correct, what we are actually doing is avoiding the embarrassment of admitting we made a mistake. The longer this goes on, the more harm is done.

I love what my good friend Linda Henman—who also works with leaders on critical decisions—says when she witnesses this: "I can't help you if you are going to be stupid." It is a clarifying statement.

Curiosity Doesn't Kill

Many companies have a habit of looking in the mirror infrequently and sometimes only after the full treatment from the marketing and PR teams. It is the professional headshot equivalent of hair and makeup. While no one expects leaders to let the public into the sausage-making room or anyone to have photos taken upon rising, we do expect the leader to have a holistic and unvarnished view of the place.

A crisis forces companies to look in the mirror. The problem with looking in the mirror is that leaders will often determine the reflection to be an aberration. The unforeseen vulnerability, the confluence of elements never before seen, a "bad apple" are explanations for dismissing the reality of what they see, and some of these explanations are, of course, plausible. In a crisis, perspective is quite naturally shortened. Once a crisis has peaked and the worst resolved, looking at the cause(s) systemically may fall to the bottom of the list of priorities.

Engaging someone whose sole purpose is to help a business improve can help leaders see things they aren't seeing, confirm some things they are seeing, and help them move more quickly. Yet, this doesn't help unless the leader will:

- Let go of the need to be right.
- Let go of the need to avoid unpleasant truths.

A senior vice president for strategy at a large company once said to me, "Sometimes your feedback and advice were like castor oil, but I knew you had our best interests at heart." He had the courage to listen. It helps tremendously that he has another wonderful attribute: he looks for cause more than blame.

Vulnerability

Over the past few years, words like *authentic* and *vulnerable* have entered the vernacular when discussing leaders, at least in some circles. Reactions range from curiosity to mocking. This is, in part, because ideas tend to get reduced far beyond a synthesis to an oversimplified distillation of easily repeated words.

What I am about to say will annoy—no, inflame—some. Some people think that repeating a word or phrase should be sufficient. They are parrots with approximately equivalent understanding. Vulnerability is too important and too complicated a concept to be prescribed like baby aspirin. Human resources people are among the worst offenders. They'll adopt a framework and cling to it for dear life, using labels to describe people instead of doing the hard work to listen, observe, and describe *relevant* behaviors.

Some adopt a set of measurement tools, which they mistakenly believe impart special powers. Then they run around with the "valid" measurement tool and give everyone a test that, while perhaps valid in the sense of content, convergence, or construct, are utterly useless in the particular setting or are being used improperly. This makes the validity studies absolutely moot. It is the equivalent of buying a perfectly good scale, then standing on it to find out how tall you are. There is some correlation between height and weight, of course, but it is not linear.

The proliferation of useless, invalid tools combined with the misuse of good methods—combined with the adulteration of the work of people who are actually qualified to do such work—has made executives cynical. It should.

Thus, concepts that smack of a "touchy-feely" philosophy are disregarded, mocked, or merely tolerated. That's if things go well. If they don't go well, an entire company will adopt a framework and, presto change-o, the whole place will speak of people in terms of a test result. This gets in the way of learning about people, but it does provide a defense against feeling vulnerable.

Vulnerability allows people to get to know one another. The value of leaders knowing the people in their company is inestimable, but it cannot be achieved without some willingness to be a human being—that is, *imperfect*.

Too often, leaders have three outbound lanes and one inbound. They work hard to get their message across but aren't listening enough or observing enough. When we listen, we realize things we didn't know and understand people in a way we hadn't before. Then we need to adapt, even change our minds. For some, that feeling of "I didn't know as much as I thought" is a painfully vulnerable feeling. For others, it's fun to open up, knowing that doing so will force them to adjust, sometimes dramatically.

Clearly, different levels of personal disclosure could be appropriate, given a particular context. Indeed, healthy individuals are more or less open, depending upon the circumstances. Even so, I know you can think of people who are stuck at one extreme or the other. Effective leaders are strategic in their thinking about when it is best to be vulnerable (admit mistakes, for example) and when they must be circumspect (such as when planning an acquisition).

Boundaries

While vulnerability is important to building trusting relationships, maintaining boundaries around it are also important. Who, after all, wants a boss who constantly shares the intimate details of his personal problems and challenges? I had that experience once and, believe me, it's not fun. On the other end of the continuum are people who can't seem to part with a shred of information that is not strictly about the work in front of them.

That's not fun either. Both create awkward exchanges, and neither is ideal. Of course, as with most things, we tend not to drive in the ideal lane all the time. We go along fine for a time, then we drift. Usually, it's fine. Indeed, being inconsistent, despite the bad rap it gets, is very human.

It's no surprise that individuals have preferences and habits regarding vulnerability and boundaries. Organizational cultures also have features related to each. This colors the relationship of people to one another and either promotes curiosity, learning, and innovation or inhibits it. If vulnerability is okay and the boundaries healthy, people can try things and succeed or fail without being psychoanalyzed as a result.

The issues with inappropriate relationships at work are legion. I'm sure you are already thinking about the obvious scenarios. The less obvious problems, however, come about from the same cause—boundaries that are in the wrong place, are too weak, or are erratic. We do not learn about boundaries by being taught explicitly; rather, we learn about them by observing, trying different behaviors, and seeing the response we get. This is a largely unconscious process, and a great deal of the learning happens in childhood. We carry our preferences, habits, and beliefs—acquired before we had much of a choice about what to adopt or reject—into our adult lives and the workplace. Here are two examples:

John, a smart, young, and ambitious man, joined Merrill Lynch a few months before me. He was a kidder from the get-go. He told jokes, made sexist remarks (always "kidding," or so he said), played practical jokes on the rest of us, and created nicknames for people—clients and colleagues alike. He could be fun, but often went too far. He lasted less than two years at Merrill Lynch, and we later learned that John's wife left him because he was unfaithful. No big surprise.

Jean, a very experienced executive, came to work for one of my clients as the head of marketing. She had quite a résumé, but her behavior at a dinner interview gave her soon-to-be new boss pause. She was pushy and demanding with the woman serving them. She asked that the time of the dinner be changed from what was offered and then asked for a driver to pick her up. The company hired her anyway, despite misgivings. Unfortunately, this behavior was just the tip of the iceberg. She lasted less than two years.

No doubt, you have thought of a few examples of your own just reading these. You may say that John was immature and Jean "entitled." I won't argue with that, but think about this—each had trouble managing his or her own behavior in a manner that suited the circumstances. Each was either clueless or careless about boundaries, or both. What these situations had in common was an inability on the part of the boss to deal with it. In John's case, his behavior was tolerated. Jean's behavior caused anguish, but the response to it was inadequate—too little, too late.

Rather than thinking in absolutes, consider the interaction of vulnerability and boundaries. A person who is flexible about when and with whom he shows vulnerability and is respectful of boundaries is ideal. The following matrix (see Figure 4.1) might help:

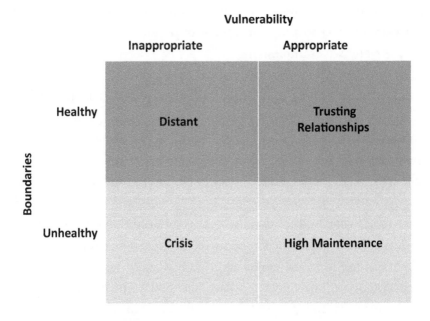

Figure 4.1 *Vulnerability and Boundaries*

Each and every person hired into a company represents a decision. The decision tells us something about the strategy, standards, and values of the people who make it. When leaders make decisions that are misaligned with what they proclaim, the company is deprived of leadership that has the courage to maintain good boundaries. When this happens, it's far better to admit a mistake than hope no one will notice.

Dangerous Rigidity

Leaders have a range of options from which to choose, despite the tendency for people to dichotomize issues when it is unnecessary. The best choices in any situation depend upon the characteristics of the specific situation, rather than on a rote procedure. Yet, time and again, we see organizations cling to what they have done in the past well beyond the point of utility.

Some leaders encourage hanging on to what was formerly effective, in the interest of stability. While "staying the course" has a seductive quality of being low risk, it is the worst kind of risk and conveys a sense of safety that is false. This is especially true when the context is unstable.

Companies that choose stability set themselves up for extinction. Eastman Kodak, Borders, Circuit City, and Polaroid are examples of companies that chose stability over change. In the face of fast-changing technology and markets, they either didn't adapt quickly enough—or at all. In contrast, IBM has evolved its business from hardware manufacturing and service to primarily consulting.

Experimentation is a necessary ingredient in innovation, something most companies seek. Great leaders make experimentation possible, though they insist that learning be an outcome. They understand that dynamics are not just in movement, but in the *potential* for movement. Too much weight on one end, and the movement won't happen. If the leader allows that weight to remain, she loses the value of the dynamics, both present and future. When a situation like this continues, an organization becomes ossified. The hardware at the fulcrum rusts, meaning that more dramatic action is needed to free up the potential. What at one point required strategic courage is now a turnaround situation or full-blown crisis.

Is there weight in your organization that prevents dynamic action? As a leader, are you creating a culture of experimentation and learning?

One leader who has remarkable ability and courage to continuously learn and improve is Susan Nethero. Nethero is the founder and former CEO of Intimacy, a specialty store for women. Dubbed "The Bra Whisperer," Nethero focused on making women feel more beautiful, comfortable, and confident. Her product may appear at first glance to be women's undergarments, but Nethero could have sold other things just as well. Why? She focused relentlessly on the need for women to find great products, and to do so with the help of a knowledgeable and sincere Intimacy employee. For Nethero, decisions about the store, the inventory, and the people were always in dynamic relationship to one another.

Death by Detail

A client once sent me a file, eighty-two pages long, and asked me to look it over. This was the "deliverable" from a big consulting firm. He asked me to review the document and tell him what I thought.

Sitting in his office the next day, I said, "The first page says it all." The first page had a graphic that depicted a particular marketplace—where this company played and where it didn't. The rest of the eighty-two page document provided proof to justify this assertion, but the strategic direction they recommended—to "own" more of this market—was on page one.

Now, the head of strategy, in whose office I was sitting, had already discussed the big idea with the president, but needed to get his peers interested in it. He asked me if he should share the file with them. I said, "No." I recommended that he instead just share the first page, and then talk about the idea. "Talk about what it would mean for your customers and your company," I told him, "and who will take this action if you don't." Finally, I explained, the most important topic to discuss is *what it would mean for the person in front of you.* My client said, "They'll want to talk about how we do it."

"Yes, of course," I replied. "That is the nature of the beast. Allowing the conversation to drift into tactics before you have two important things in place will derail it in short order. What are the two things? First, a picture of what the future will be if the strategy is implemented. Second, what it will mean to the person you are speaking with when that happens."

Why did I say this to my client? Because of a simple fact of human behavior—facts make us think, but emotion gives us fuel to act. And facts can get in the way of enthusiasm.

Stunted by Strategy

A very common issue I hear from senior executives about their subordinates is that they are too tactical. I'm asked if Jill or Robert should be shipped off to Wharton or Kellogg or some other school to study strategic planning. Sometimes this is a good option, but it depends. What does it depend upon? It depends upon whether or not the individual is a strategic thinker who would benefit from exposure to certain methods, or if the person needs to shift his thinking from generally tactical to more strategic. These are very different issues, though "send them to school" is most often the answer.

What's the harm, you ask? The harm is that for people who need to think more strategically, teaching them a method/process/framework will further inhibit their ability to think differently. They will acquire a new vocabulary, hear about other companies, and meet peers from different industries, businesses, and geographies. The last thing in this list has been demonstrated to be one of the key benefits of education of this type. That's not a bad thing, but a glorified networking opportunity may not be what you thought you were paying for.

Darren, a very successful man who rose from an entry-level position in his company to become president of a business unit, had a mastery of operational matters that would impress anyone. He knew the ins and outs of his business and could walk into a location and tell you within three minutes what was going right and what was going wrong. These are good qualities for a head of operations, but not so great for someone responsible for overseeing all the functions of the business. Darren should have been able to answer strategic questions such as:

- Who are our customers of the future?
- What demographic changes will impact us?
- Do we know what our vulnerabilities are? How do we know?

This expert in the past and present, and a very fine human being as well, had a hard time dealing with conceptual material, abstraction, or innovation. He dismissed ideas brought to him from other businesses, saying, "They aren't in our business." He couldn't see analogies. Sad but true.

The strategy workshop was eye opening for him. To his great credit, he opened himself up to the professors, other executives in attendance, and the material. He read everything assigned, listened intently, and asked questions. He struggled to apply the concepts but he kept at it. Later, he told me that he was afraid of appearing stupid, but he figured this was the place to do it. The value of his experience was this: he became a far more astute leader because he could ask different questions, and he was no longer afraid of not knowing something.

Darren didn't fall into the trap of thinking that a set of procedures, a template, or a checklist of items made one a great strategist. He didn't need to become *the* strategist. He needed to lead his team to think strategically. In that way, he was among the most strategic of all.

Customer Behavior Doesn't Lie

How many times have you experienced the following?

- Someone insisting on giving you unnecessary "background"?
- A lengthy response to a question you did not ask?

- A detailed, verbal résumé of someone whom you just met in a social setting?
- Multiple electronic files in support of an opinion?

No one is listening! Absolutely no one. They may be looking at you and may even thank you for being thorough, but you must know this—they aren't listening! The reason is not that a particular percentage of information is nonverbal, or that people need to hear something so many times to remember it. Those oft-repeated "facts" aren't true anyway. People aren't listening to you because what you are saying is not important to them. That's the secret. We spend too much time yakking about what others don't care about. It doesn't make us bad, rude, or mean. It means that we—you or me, or whoever—are blathering on and not responding to the need that is on our audience's mind at the time.

How do you know if you are talking to but not connecting with your customers, employees, colleagues, or prospects? You have to pay attention to behavior, both yours and the other person's. Are you doing all the talking? Is he? Are you asking questions and then listening to the answers? Are you learning about what is important to the person?

Online data are powerful precisely because they are a record of what people have done. This type of data, call it "big data" if you insist, is generated when people do things online such as search, select, click on a link, abandon a process, complete a process, buy something, look at something, and much more. Before you get too paranoid, much of this data is aggregate data. Mostly, people looking at it don't care about individuals; they care about patterns and trends. The advantage and the disadvantage of this data is that it's historical. The question is, can this data predict the future?

Meanwhile, companies are still doing surveys, both live and online, in an astonishing number. You can't rent a car, stay in a hotel, fly, or shop without also prompting a survey. My favorite line about surveys came from a Delta flight attendant. She was absolutely terrific during the flight, very good natured and funny. As we were approaching the Atlanta airport on a Friday afternoon, she got most of the dog-tired passengers to laugh by reminding us that we would receive a survey from Delta. She said that if we had a wonderful flight, she hoped we would fill it out. If not, she said, "Please delete the e-mail."

Of course, if only happy customers respond, Delta doesn't learn what it wants to know. Nor does Saks Fifth Avenue get the feedback it needs when salespeople ask you to fill out a survey, but to tell them beforehand if there is any reason that you can't give them the highest rating on all the questions. You haven't even seen the questions!

The Courage to Let Go

The courage to let go of a failed strategy, product, service, business unit, physical facility, or employee is one of the most underutilized actions, across the board. Strategic courage is exemplified by letting go. If we think it's difficult to let go of employees, it may be even more difficult to let go of customers or an entire segment.

While meeting with a client who worked for Ritz-Carlton, I learned about a segment of their guest population that was chronically dissatisfied. I don't mean they experienced minor issues such as room service taking too long or not enough towels by the pool. I'm speaking about customers who complain about multiple things—every single visit—and demand recompense. She told me that one customer in particular had accrued a large number of free nights simply by routinely complaining about the service he received. The Ritz-Carlton employee was frustrated that her manager would not "fire" this customer, who was not only a complainer but, in her words, was "mean and nasty." This man berated the staff and did it in front of other customers.

It seems obvious that this customer needs to be cut loose. But what of others who are less demanding, yet still create more work and discord than they are worth? What of customers who won't pay the fees your company sets?

Netflix is dealing with this issue, again. In 2014, it raised prices and was resoundingly criticized. The company backed off the increase and kept the

$7.99 per month fee in place for two years for existing customers. New customers paid $9.99. Now, two years later, Netflix raised the fee for those who had been "grandfathered." Again, there is a huge and negative reaction to the price hike. As Jim Cramer pointed out, it's tough to imagine that $2 per month would make someone leave a service like this. I agree, but customer behavior doesn't lie. Now Netflix has a choice to make. If it does not chase customers who cancel rather than pay more, Netflix mustn't criticize these customers. Letting go works best if you let go and put your energies elsewhere rather than trying to prove why the other guy is wrong.

Note

1. Lee Dranikoff, Tim Koller, and Antoon Schneider, "Divestiture: Strategy's Missing Link," May 2005, accessed February 15, 2017, https://hbr.org/2002/05/divestiture-strategys-missing-link.

PART II

Judgment

It slightly worries me that when people find a problem, they rush to judgment of what to do.

—Janet Yellen

CHAPTER 5

Grounded in Values

Susan Nethero's mother and grandmother provided her with powerful models of elegance. They dressed well, paid attention to fashion, and encouraged Nethero to do the same. She says they were elegant, and when she says it, the look on her face shows admiration and pure delight.

As Nethero matured, her mother realized that the intimate apparel options available to her daughter in their town were not going to work. The solution? Trips to New York City, where specialty stores were very different from the department stores closer to home. They had better products, broader selection and, most important, women who were expert in helping to choose and fit their customers. These stores' inventory included products from Europe that were well made and beautiful. The salespeople understood how the products were constructed, what brand and style was better for whom, and how to fit women properly. Their expertise was as important as the products themselves.

Years later, Nethero and her husband, David, moved to Atlanta. Fortuitously, this event occurred at the same time she felt the urge to exercise her entrepreneurial muscle. She knew from her own experience—and the experience of her girlfriends—that the process of buying a bra usually followed one of two paths. Either a woman expected good products and great service, and was almost always left disappointed, or she gave in, bought something that she felt was "good enough," and moved on.

Nethero knew what few others did—that undergarments should make us look and feel better. She started her new business with these values at the center of everything she did—actually, they were more like convictions:

- Women deserve well-fitting underpinnings.
- Beauty should not be sacrificed in the name of utility.
- What we wear that no one sees matters to how we feel.
- The experience of buying intimate apparel should be rewarding.

These beliefs guided Nethero's decisions as she built her business. She knew that the location of her first store was pivotal. She chose Phipps Plaza in Atlanta, where the anchor department store was, and still is, Saks Fifth Avenue. Phipps is a popular choice for high-end shoppers. On any given day, you are likely to run across someone famous. I once sat across from boxing great Floyd Mayweather in the shoe department. This was a wise decision on Nethero's part, and a great location for the first Intimacy store.

Ethical Conviction

Nethero's store had to be beautiful, the people working there needed to be experts, and the customer experience had to be so rewarding that women would tell all their friends. Nethero is not a woman who does things half-heartedly. She is enthusiasm personified, but she knows it takes more than that to start a business.

An important aspect of Nethero's character and thinking style is that she looks at things holistically. It's not that transactions and short-term wins aren't her style; they actually violate her sense of ethics. Win-win isn't enough for her. Win-win can be an exchange, but for Nethero, relationships are what create the opportunity for mutual gain to go on and on. The value is financial *and* relational, monetary *and* psychological.

Nethero made sure the products stocked at Intimacy were extraordinary, the store beautiful, and the staff both knowledgeable and sincere in their purpose. What was their purpose? Selling bras, of course, but far more. Their task was to create an environment where women felt understood and valued. When a woman left the store, she was to feel more beautiful and confident than when she walked in. If she bought nothing, the experience would draw her back in. If she bought one item, the joy in it would lead her back.

How do you get employees to convey something so subjective and, dare I say it, emotional? You do it by treating them well. All the employees at Intimacy were full time. All of them learned from Nethero, whose expertise eventually earned her the title "the Bra Whisperer." Employees were treated like professionals, and only those who would take sincere joy in helping customers would work well at Intimacy. *Teamwork* and *culture* are often-used words in every business today, but for Nethero, they are imperatives to be built and protected by the leader.

All new ventures could be considered high stakes. Nethero's venture was particularly so because Intimacy promised a very different experience for its customers than that offered by competitors. She knew her team had to do more than build brand identity, they had to build equity by delivering on the promise. Nethero set up in a high-end mall, decorated the place beautifully, and stocked the store with beautiful and extremely well-made garments. However, if the actual customer experience didn't match the look and the promise, Intimacy would fail. Nethero knew it.

Triple Play

When the stakes are high, Nethero amps up her engagement with colleagues and partners. She looks for those who share her vision and are sincerely seeking it for their own sake. Once she knows what the other person will get, she can form a powerful alliance that creates mutual gain.

Thinking about what is in the interest of others is fundamental to Nethero's success, but it is no act—she is completely sincere. After the terrorist attacks on the United States on September 11, 2001, Nethero realized that there would be a slowdown in the economy. The shock would cause people to freeze up, even if temporarily. She went to her suppliers and said "I'll take inventory now, but I want a greater discount than usual." She made sure they understood the benefit to them, not just the details of her ask. She got what she asked for.

Nethero says, "You have to ask for what you want, but you also need to give people a reason to help you." Sometimes that reason is financial, and other times it is emotional. For years, she had been telling friends and colleagues that she was going to open a store on Madison Avenue. Shopping in specialty stores in Manhattan with her mother and grandmother left an indelible and very positive mark on her when she was a girl.

Eventually, Nethero heard about a store in a great location that the owner was ready to sell. It was a perfect. She met the woman and spent a lot of time with her, learning about what the store meant to her. The woman wanted more money than Nethero and her husband could rationalize for their budget, and so they were forced to say no. But they didn't say no to the store owner in a transactional way—they did it in a way that respected the relationship they had built with the woman. Two years later, the woman called them. They quickly struck a deal and opened their new store on Madison Avenue.

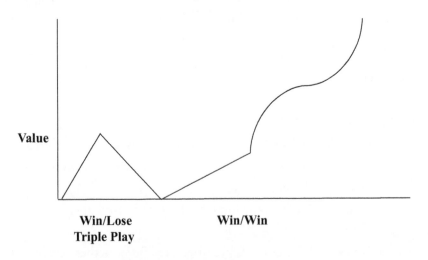

Figure 5.1 *The Triple Play*

Nethero is a master of the triple play (see Figure 5.1):

- Ask for what you want.
- Understand what the other person needs.
- Invest in the relationship.

The Oprah Effect

Then, just as Intimacy was beginning to gain traction in the marketplace, Oprah happened. That is, Nethero was invited to appear on *The Oprah Winfrey Show*. After her first appearance on *Oprah*, the Intimacy website exploded with 1.6 million hits. But that was just the beginning. Nethero appeared on *Oprah* four more times. She was also on the *Today* show and others, but Oprah made Nethero and her business a hit. We usually think of high stakes when there is a risk of going out of business, and that's true, but success brings great risk too, if you aren't ready for it.

After she appeared on *Oprah*, the floodgates opened. Nethero knew that if the inventory wasn't sufficient or the service suffered, the flood of people and the goodwill she had generated would evaporate. She might very well be worse off than if she hadn't been on *Oprah* in the first place. Nethero and her team quickly set up a system for scheduling appointments to make sure that when women came to the store to shop, they would have the attention they deserved. To make that happen, Nethero had to slow down just long enough to figure out a system. It may have taken no more than two minutes, but she had to hit "pause," pay attention to what needed to be done, and make a decision.

Timing and Patience

As important as decisiveness and quick action can be, patience and a sense of timing are equally significant. More crippling than failure is the belief that what led to success in one scenario will lead to success in another.

Overgeneralizing happens when we apply something correctly in one situation and, believing we have uncovered a universal truth, apply it in another. We force fit a fact, a technique, or a methodology regardless of the situation. Before you decide that people who do this are stupid, let me stop you. This is not stupid; rather, it is a human tendency. It is a way to simplify our interactions with the world around us, and it happens outside our awareness unless we force this tendency into consciousness.

Overgeneralizing is what causes a leader who achieves stunning results in one high-stakes situation to be a poor advisor to others. To lead effectively—especially when there is much at risk—leaders need to see a situation, look for patterns, *and* look for distinctions. With those three pieces in place, judgment about what to do improves. This requires intentional thought.

Pattern recognition, more than instinct, permits leaders to make superior judgments that look to others like a nearly mystical insight. The more experience a person has with a phenomenon, the better she becomes at recognizing patterns. A surgeon doing her nine hundredth appendectomy will know more quickly if something is amiss than a medical resident doing her third. A mother who knows her two-year-old child is sick by recognizing subtle signs may have been baffled by the cries of a newborn. A director who has worked on many CEO successions is more valuable than the one who worked on just one, especially if it was successful. This sort of history builds up a belief in technique rather than judgment.

Susan Nethero was patient about the store on Madison Avenue. Patrick Brennan was patient as he got to know the recently acquired DSC. Rachel Moore took the time to get to know people at the Los Angeles Music Center. Each of these people uses patience just as much as facts, and each values what can be achieved when it is applied at the right time.

When the *Challenger* experienced multiple delays, frustration built within the NASA launch team and "go fever" took over. Patience in situations such as these is hard to come by—it's as though the supply has run out. In high-stakes situations, leaders cannot afford to run out of the ability to hit pause. It takes intentional effort to get our brains to switch from the automatic response to a more deliberate way of thinking.

In his book *Thinking, Fast and Slow*, Dr. Daniel Kahneman describes two specific modes of thought—what he terms System 1 and System 2. System 1 thinking is fast and instinctive, and requires less effort. It is also more emotional and, when the stakes are high, more dangerous. System 2 thinking is more logical but is also slower. Human beings don't like to slow down to deliberate if we think we know—if we've *got it*. We can be downright cranky and argumentative. These emotions get in our way. In our effort to avoid discomfort, we often opt for quick judgments. When they are right, all is well. When they are wrong, it's trouble. Giving in to our tendencies may be human nature, but it can also lead to crisis. When leaders value only "going fast," it can be tough to prevent them from running off the road, even only occasionally.

Belief in the Unseen

Kahneman's model of thinking is not something you can see. System 1 and System 2 don't show up on an MRI, but the effects are observable. Think for a moment about the things that you cannot directly observe but are important to your happiness and health, things like achievement, satisfaction, love, acceptance, admiration, friendship, respect, mutual regard, and so forth. These are things that are important to humans—not all in equal measure for everyone, but they are common. We can observe the artifacts or residue of their action, but not the phenomena directly. Achievement—for example, in the form of high school or college diplomas—comes to mind. Love might take the form of a wedding ring and friendship may be evidenced by people showing up at our birthday party.

At work, we are usually trying to achieve a goal, but the feeling we have when we succeed or fail is an experience, not a thing. We know relationships through our experience with them. Few artifacts are as convincing as the experience itself.

While our ways of thinking are also temporal, we can observe our own process and that of others. This cognitive process of reflection is a key way that adults learn, even when what we are learning is about how we think, what our default assumptions are, and our tendencies to see or not see particular things. When leaders place a value on this reflective process, they allow others to shift gears, use different lenses, and make better decisions.

Evolving Judgment

Chris Dods, the CEO of Clean Earth, Inc., is a leader whom I have known for more than ten years. Dods has always been a successful person—first as a student, and later as a high school athlete good enough to attract the attention of the Naval Academy.

When I met Dods, he was with ARAMARK Uniform Services. He performed, no doubt about that. Achievement is his middle name. But all was not smooth sailing (pun intended). Dods ran afoul of some of his superiors, who didn't like *how* he did things. They had no argument about *what* he achieved, but did not always appreciate his methods.

After a time with ARAMARK, Dods left and later joined a company owned by a private equity firm, the CEO of which was an ex-McKinsey guy. This was fine with Dods—an analytical, McKinsey-like approach is something he is comfortable with and can do easily. But Dods does not like to do things just because someone says so. He detests bureaucracy and irrelevant activities, and rebels against them. More than merely disliking them, he places a high value on streamlining, for himself and his company. In this new company, he experienced a similar clash of values. His priorities are about getting the job done in the most pragmatic way. His boss valued a certain protocol. Disagreements like these were, by now, familiar.

Later, when Dods was considering his next professional move, he met the owners of Clean Earth. By this time, he had come to a different understanding of his own style. He was reflective enough to look back, and was able to be honest with himself about what works and what doesn't. Dods may be stubborn, but he's a realist.

One thing he realized was that, while he was able to manage details, he didn't like it. Keeping his personal level of annoyance low would benefit everyone, so he created an environment that would enable him to put his energy toward activities that would be most beneficial. He was also thinking about his focus on results. Focusing on results without doing the work to create the right conditions would result in neither optimal nor sustainable performance. Importantly, the people who don't like your methods might have a point. Ironically, Clean Earth is in the sustainability business, and even the company's strategic plan is dubbed the *sustainability plan*.

Dods knew that his job wasn't just to deliver the goods; it mattered *how* he did it. This was a major change for him—a 180-degree turn. He realized that if he understood what others needed and wanted, he would be able to do more, get better results, and make the people around him happier and more motivated.

In this way, Dods is like Susan Nethero, Patrick Brennan, Rachel Moore, and other leaders I've yet to talk about. These leaders all know what is important, and they have the discipline to reach out to others, to listen, to learn, and to build relationships. The relationships needed are of various types and none are all encompassing. Judith Viorst wrote in her book *Necessary Losses*, "Even the best of friends are friends in spots."[1] I recall reading that and feeling stunned. Aren't friends supposed to be friends in all weather? That, it turns out, is a very rare thing. Expecting it is to be so is a recipe for heartache.

Business relationships are similar. They have their spots—their *spaces*. The IT person doesn't give you advice about where to build your next manufacturing plant. He may have input and pieces of information, but he doesn't have the full picture. That doesn't make the person fair-weather anything.

Relationships are what allow us to learn together, form partnerships, be forgiven when we make mistakes, and hear criticism. A relationship that is strong tolerates disagreement. It is the weak ones that break in conflict rather than bend to allow resolution. An organization where relationships are weak and ideas quashed is brittle and far more likely to end up in a crisis than one where people can tell you there is smoke before the fire engulfs it. When relationships are strong, people are more willing to "take the hill" together, whether the hill is literal or metaphorical.

Motivation Is Fuel

Soon after Chris Dods took over his new role at Clean Earth, his assistant came to him to resign. Dods asked what the issue was, and she told him she just didn't want to come to the office so early. He asked her, "What time do you want to come in?" She told him and he said, "Well, then do that." She was in disbelief. Her issue was not difficult to resolve, especially because her boss doesn't like practices that have no practical value any more than did his assistant. What if he had focused the conversation on her resignation, tried to make her feel guilty, or tried to cajole her without any additional information?

Dods realized that learning more about what others expect and need—whether they are colleagues or not—allows him to do more of what he is trying to do, not less. The bonus is, when he can give someone more of what they want, he gets stronger relationships with colleagues, customers and, yes, even competitors. The change in his focus from *only results matter* to *if you create the right conditions, the results will come*, is profound. It is a shift in his values that is, he'd tell you, for the better.

What Dods does is: he pays attention. The things he pays attention to have changed over the years, as has how much value he gives to which things. Because he is paying attention differently, he better understands what people want control over and he is willing to offer it, where possible. This pays off with almost everyone. External rewards work only for a time, and sometimes not at all. Offering a reward for something that a person does naturally because it is intrinsically rewarding can actually cause the person to engage in the behavior less often.[2] This feeling of reward is emotional, and, as we know, emotion is the gas for behavior. It's far easier to look for it and match the motivation to the job than it is to try to motivate people. Sadly, a lot of money and effort is wasted trying to create motivation when it simply needs to be discovered and unleashed.

Unethical Dilemmas

A dilemma that leaders sometimes find themselves in is the one that emerges when they discover employees doing things that clearly violate their company values and ethics. Leaders at VW, GM, and Countrywide all faced this dilemma and failed—putting their companies at great risk. And in the fall of 2016, Wells Fargo joined the list after federal regulators and the Los Angeles City Attorney's office publicly revealed that Wells Fargo employees opened up to two million bogus deposit and credit card accounts without the knowledge of its customers. The CEO of Wells Fargo, John Stumpf, admitted that he "feels accountable" for the transgressions, but explained that some employees didn't honor the bank's values.[3]

Okay, Mr. Stumpf, we understand your need to say that. But here's the thing, you didn't have your finger on the pulse or, to be exact, the *right* pulse. Once unethical acts come to light, you don't have much time to recover. Indeed, Stumpf landed on the Senate Banking Committee's agenda less than two weeks after the issue became public.

Whether you are John Stumpf, or any other leader—CEO or not—this is what you need to know about handling a crisis that calls your values into question.

- **Look beneath the surface.** Don't wait for your feet to get wet to tell you the tide is in. Spreadsheets and dashboards tell you what has happened in the past—they don't tell you *how* it happened. Doing this takes patience and discipline. Stumpf blamed individual employees, rogue actors. This argument doesn't hold up. In December 2013, the *LA Times* reported questionable sales practices, and in May 2015, the LA city attorney filed a lawsuit in which it was alleged that Wells

Fargo had been aggressive in pushing employees to open accounts, even if they committed fraud to do so.

- **Understand how this will impact your customers.** If you address only the manifest issue, you'll look shallow. "Gee, we're sorry for the mistakes and we'll fix them." Great. Do you realize that my trust in you just went down by about 75 percent? Speak to that! Act with that in mind. On September 13, 2016, Wells Fargo announced it would end all product sales goals in retail banking—starting on January 1, 2017.[4] What? This is not the time for patience; it is time to take decisive action in line with your remarks.

- **Do not excuse or minimize wrongdoing.** Do not be euphemistic in your language. Don't blame a "few bad apples"—no one believes you, especially given the numbers of employees (more than five thousand) reportedly fired by Wells Fargo for wrongdoing. When a leader tries to make a pattern look like a series of random events, he is not fooling us.

- **Look in the mirror.** If you, a leader, have been satisfied with knowing only *what* but nothing about *how*, you are part of the problem. A leader needs to know how the organization works and how the results came to be, not just what they are. *Counterintuitively, this applies when things are going well just as much as when they are not.* If a leader doesn't know why things are happening, what the cause is, his judgments about what to do will be right only accidentally. Even after some bad actors were identified at Wells Fargo, the systemic cause was ignored.

Have Character, Don't Be One

Just as people have a strong tendency to see cause in correlation when none exists, we can be blind to patterns that will tell us far more than the pieces. When trying to influence others, it is sometimes effective to imply cause or to draw attention to an array of data to prevent others from seeing the information that lies just beyond our recognition. These things can be unwitting or intentional and done to promote a sound idea—or manipulate for destructive purposes. It is the stuff from which propaganda is made and about which much is written. Fortunately, by keeping earnest people around us, we can be challenged and corrected. That works so long as we don't punish them for doing so.

A CEO I knew some years ago was known to be a tyrant. What made him so hard to deal with is he didn't look like a tyrant or yell or scream. What did he do? He put people in the deep freeze. Not literally, of course, but he had a way of ignoring people that made them feel insignificant. If you want to demotivate people, a good way to do it is to deprive them of any interaction. It is painful and demotivating for people to be ignored.

In the case of this person, the board eventually got tired of hearing how bad a leader he was and fired him. Before they fired him, however, they hired a coach to help him. He mocked the coach, was late for their meetings, and sent him articles about how coaches are charlatans (okay, some are). The coach declared that he could not help the CEO. He was right. The board, in hindsight, wondered how they had been so wrong about him. They were deeply regretful about it. They were also painfully aware that they had assumed the CEO shared their values. The board evaluated the relationship between themselves and him as pretty good. This judgment led them to assume that his relationships with others were also good enough. The board didn't use bad judgment intentionally, but they were not asking the right questions, nor were they interacting with the senior management team enough to evaluate the quality of leadership the CEO was providing.

As with all situations like this one, after a leader is gone, more comes to light. The board realized just how controlling this man had been and how stifled the organization was as a result. Fortunately, the successor was a far less arrogant person who did a much better job. Even so, the board adopted some new, and quite good, practices to ensure that they weren't governing from such a distance. The new practices better reflect the values the board holds and leads them to make different judgments and, therefore, different decisions. They have done far more than say what they value; they discuss how to recognize it when they see it and what they will do when leaders deviate. This is the way to make the values a meaningful aspect of an organization.

Notes

1. Judith Viorst, *Necessary Losses: The Loves, Illusions, Dependencies, and Impossible Expectations That All of Us Have to Give Up in Order to Grow*. New York: Free Press (1998), p. 183.
2. Jeremy Dean, "How Rewards Can Backfire and Reduce Motivation," *Psyblog*, October 2009, accessed February 15, 2017, www.spring.org.uk/2009/10/how-rewards-can-backfire-and-reduce-motivation.php.
3. Emily Glazer, "How Wells Fargo's High-Pressure Sales Culture Spiraled Out of Control," *Wall Street Journal*, September 16, 2016.
4. "Wells Fargo to Eliminate Product Sales Goals for Retail Bankers," press release, accessed February 15, 2017, www.wellsfargo.com/about/press/2016/eliminate-sales-goals_0913/.

CHAPTER 6

Bold Discernment

I confess a fascination with Warby Parker, the eyeglasses company. In his terrific book *Originals*, Adam Grant writes about the company, the founders, and his regrettable decision not to invest in the start-up. Grant confesses, "I was stuck in the default mindset of how glasses were traditionally bought and sold."[1] While his thinking was mired in the status quo, we can thank him for not only admitting it, but also for examining the decisions of the founders that led to their success.

In starting the company, the founders first rejected the default position that Grant admits trapped him. The default position is something we accept as "just the way it is." Questioning this mind-set can lead to creativity and innovation, just as entrepreneur Sara Blakely did when starting her company, Spanx.

This status quo–busting thinking also fueled another Atlanta-based entrepreneur, Lance Ledbetter. He started Dust-to-Digital to make the genre of "roots" music accessible to more listeners. Previously, the effort it took to find and acquire this obscure genre of music required research, tenacity, and special equipment on which to play it. Ledbetter just couldn't believe that it had to be that way. Now, it isn't. Dust-to-Digital puts rare and old music into the hands of adventurous listeners. More than that, the company has created *new* listeners.

Warby Parker, Spanx, and Dust-to-Digital have all achieved success by rejecting the default position, and then having the courage to take the risky paths to achieving their unique visions of the future. Their ability to discern a different path led them to create something different and seize the opportunity. In each case, the company's focus was on providing something that was new, or providing something old in a new way.

Breaking the B-School Rules

In his book, Grant describes his own evaluation of the Warby Parker founders' (Andrew Hunt, Dave Gilboa, Jeff Raider, and Neil Blumenthal) plans to keep day jobs while they started the company. He isn't alone. We tend to value the "all-in" posture more than the "stick-our-toe-in" position. But keeping risk low has distinct advantages. One notable plus is having less worry about going bust. If you aren't risking it all, you can take the time you need to gather information and make decisions. The types of decisions that need deliberate thought (System 2 in Kahneman's theory) are not done best under time pressure. Deliberate, discerning thought is needed when we are in new territory or when what we are working on is complex.

According to Grant, other factors contributed to Warby Parker's success, including hedging, testing ideas, and seeking feedback. The process of seeking broad feedback started early on with the founders testing the name, the website design, and functionality. As the company grew, employees were included in discussions, asked to make suggestions, and invited to participate in the evaluation of ideas. The genius of this is not only in allowing people to feel like a part of the company, but also in giving them experience in evaluation—increasing their base of knowledge and ability to be discerning.

The notion of involving employees in the process of decision making works especially well when the employees are curious and motivated to learn. The process of developing pattern recognition is often unconscious. Bringing the learning into consciousness not only enhances it for ourselves, but also makes us better able to share what we know with others. In an environment that applauds curiosity, continuous improvement, and use of the best ideas from wherever they arise offer a powerful competitive advantage. To capture this advantage, leaders must give up the idea that they are the source of all organizational knowledge and the seat of all decisions. Risk is significantly reduced when leaders intentionally challenge their own thinking. How to do this is not self-evident, but it is an important method for distinguishing between inspiration and insanity.

Distortion by Cynicism

Keith was a very likeable fellow who had made his way from GE, where he worked in finance, to a technology company, and then to a business that relied on technology to deliver a service. He was the CEO of this privately owned company whose investors were a public company and two wealthy individuals. His Achilles heel was an inability to make tough calls. He just couldn't do it. The way he dealt with conflict or dissatisfied employees was to bribe them. He was utterly unable to discern the disastrous consequences of his decisions, most notably those he sidestepped.

What prevented him from making tough decisions? His cynical beliefs. If he fired a chief financial officer, he would need a new one. A new chief financial officer might be the wrong person, might upset the applecart, or might find out just how much trouble the business was in. At least the current chief financial officer kept his mouth shut in the board meetings and let the CEO decide what to share.

Keith was so tentative and insecure that changes in his senior team terrified him. The leaders who reported to him were, consciously or not, wise to this. They dumped all manner of business and personal issues at his feet, and he took up the burden. No matter how difficult, burdensome, or sticky things got, he took on whatever people pushed his way. This makes him sound pretty dumb, I realize. He was not. He had great analytical reasoning ability, speed, and considerable knowledge. He had an Ivy League education.

The issue here was emotional. Keith's cynicism kept him from seeing things clearly. The investors were meddling. Some senior executives had a back channel to particular investors and were undermining him. The customers wanted to be bribed into opening accounts that they would close as soon as they could without penalty. In his mind, everyone had an angle. However, he didn't see his own game until someone called him on it. It took an outsider to do that, as is often the case.

My Baloney Is Better than Yours

Until such time that someone recognizes that things are going wrong and speaks up, people who are perpetrating a falsehood get bolder and bolder. They are convinced—and become more so over time—that the story they tell is actually true. What they recognized as a lie early on becomes defensible. This allows them to perpetuate whatever it is they are doing.

The danger? People like this come to believe their own story about themselves. They may feel infallible and take on wild risks. Examples include Bernie Madoff, Ken Lay, and Jeffrey Skilling at Enron; L. Dennis Kozlowski and Mark Swartz at Tyco; and, most recently, those who employed the wildly ill-advised tactics in the retail business at Wells Fargo. When wrongdoers are found out, we can be shocked—especially when those who do the wrong seem to violate their own stated values. Included in Wells Fargo's lengthy document on its values is this statement: "We value what's right for our customers in everything we do."[2] Reasonable people understand that companies don't live up to lofty statements such as this every moment of every day. What we find unacceptable is denial, rationalizing, and trying to pass off baloney as tenderloin.

Keith's behavior as CEO was motivated by his own self-interest, though not in the most obvious way. Yes, he loved private jets and public appearances with top officials and celebrities, but what drove him most powerfully was fear of losing status. For him, failing was not temporary—it was fatal. So he did everything he could to avoid it, even lie to his board.

In contrast, successful people who are more grounded and less defensive, and who have a growth mind-set, talk about failures and setbacks as inevitable. Not that anyone sets out to fail, but it happens to everyone. The danger is in viewing failures as permanent. If failures are permanent to us, and if we dramatize the consequences of failure, we are bound to avoid facing up to them.

Deadly Overconfidence

When I was a stockbroker, I encountered a great deal of overconfidence in my clients—and among my colleagues. I can't say which was more damaging, but my curiosity about the effect of emotion on decisions has been driving me ever since. Following are a few examples of this overconfidence.

A university professor in a business school convinced himself that he could make money by trading options. Not something on the conservative side, however, such as selling covered calls (when you own a stock and sell the right for someone to buy it from you before a certain time at a given price). No, he wanted to buy and sell options using an approach that was far riskier. The professor was in his fifties at the time and he had some money, so his scheme didn't raise red flags in the compliance department.

He traded options rather successfully for more than a year, and you can imagine what this did to his confidence. Yes, it went up—a lot. He thought he had found "the secret" to investing success. So on he went, trading and slowly growing his investments. Then a downturn wiped him out. Not completely, but he took some major losses. What do you think happened to the professor's confidence in his strategy? Did it go up or down?

It went up.

He doubled down on his beliefs, getting angry at the market. The professor wouldn't listen to our advice, and he ultimately took his account elsewhere so he wouldn't have to listen to our warnings any longer. This was a relief to us. It was hard to watch someone lose so badly while continuing to do what had created the risk in the first place.

Another client, a woman in her sixties, had a relatively small account (less than $500,000). Her money was in very secure investments, but the growth was, as you might expect, slow. When her son-in-law was fired from his job, he decided to open a retail store and asked her to invest. She liquidated her account and gave all the money to him.

Neither the professor nor the retired woman was unsure about their decision. Neither of them saw their choices as high risk. You probably see it differently. I certainly did, and I still do.

Wired for Overconfidence

Why are stories like this more than curiosities? Because they are examples of the very human tendency to be overconfident. This confidence is best described by Daniel Kahneman in *Thinking, Fast and Slow.* Observed Kahneman, "emotional, cognitive, and social factors that support exaggerated optimism are a heady brew, which sometimes leads people to take risks that they would avoid if they knew the odds."[3]

I discuss overconfidence in chapter 3 of this book. Kahneman describes it from multiple angles, as the previous quote suggests. Interestingly, the human tendency toward overconfidence shows up as a resistance to the very idea. Yet, mistakes happen because of it. Sometimes disasters are caused by it, yet, resist we do.

The best way to reduce the risk from being overly optimistic is to challenge ourselves to think of what we haven't thought of. That sounds impossible. The founders of Warby Parker used feedback to help with this. Companies use various methods to gather information, and sometimes they pay attention to it. But the question remains, what information are they gathering, from what source, and how?

A client told me about some "market research" they were planning, and as they described it in a meeting I could scarcely believe what I was hearing. They were going to survey their customers. I asked, "How will you find out what people are thinking who are not your customers, but could be?" You see the problem. They had narrowed the inquiry in such a way as to seriously reduce what they would learn. The CEO had some rather pointed questions for the executive responsible for this.

Contrast the Warby Parker way of gathering information with that of the organization I just mentioned. One is outward facing, the other inward. One is actively trying to learn, while the other is insular and protective to the point that they made a point of trying not to. Once a company understands the difference and takes a good, unvarnished look at itself, it can make great improvements. To do otherwise only magnifies risk.

Thumbs Down on Rules of Thumb

A rule of thumb is a principle meant to simplify or guide understanding, a shortcut. For example:

- Retirement savings should equal ten times your highest salary.
- People retain only 6 percent of what they hear.
- CEOs hired from the outside will bring fresh ideas.
- Extraverts talk more than introverts.
- Substance abuse treatment succeeds when the person "hits rock bottom."
- People are "coin operated"—a particularly distasteful and untrue example.

It's easy to see how these things can help us. Shortcuts simplify and save time. Most of all, they save effort—*thinking* effort. When the stakes are low, shortcuts aren't a problem. When there is time to correct a mistake, or if the negative effect of a mistake is likely to be minor, shortcuts can be okay. Yet, seek shortcuts we do, even when the stakes are high.

Each of us is bombarded with all sorts of inputs, information, and data from a variety of different sources every day, some of it reliable and some not. If we didn't look for ways to simplify and filter this near-constant torrent, our heads would collectively explode. But we don't seek rules of thumb for this reason alone. We do it because our minds are hard at work on an unconscious level, organizing information. We simply can't analyze every single thing that happens during the course of the day, verify every bit of data, or know as much as we wish before making major decisions.

A rule of thumb presents the danger of quickly becoming an assumption that we never test—a permanent part of our worldview. Look at the decisions people in a family make about where to live, where to shop, what type of phone to buy, what car to drive, and where and how to buy it. Should you have a home free and clear of debt, or should you take advantage of the financial leverage a mortgage provides? Violate the family norms and you'll have to spend energy discussing it, and maybe even defending your choices. How many holiday dinners have you attended where people talk endlessly about how they traveled, via what route, on what airline, and why someone else's way is better? My way is faster, cheaper, less of a hassle. In the end, the message is, "You are wrong."

When shared across an organization, the rules of thumb that become assumptions may be harmful, but they can also create a high-value culture. What if the assumption is that a customer on the phone or in front of you takes priority over stocking shelves? What if the assumption is that enthusiasm and goodwill are part of the environment? Shared assumptions are challenging because they are often unconscious. Making them conscious takes discernment and, sometimes, help. But here's the trick—knowing what the assumptions are won't change them. If the behavior of the leaders does not match the behaviors they want to see in others, the result is the worst type of culture.

Zappos and the Four Seasons

Marketers constantly think about brand identity—what the brand stands for, its promise—and brand equity—that is, does it deliver?

A well-known and positive example of a brand that hits it out of the park on both counts is online shoe retailer Zappos. A few years ago, I bought a beautiful pair of boots from Zappos and, as usual, they showed up quickly. I was so thrilled that I put them on immediately, and . . . darn, they were tight!

Reluctantly, I called Zappos and said, "These boots are too tight." What ensued was a twenty-minute conversation, during which I tried the boots on again. Then, I walked around my house, taking care not to scratch the soles of the boots. The entire time, the Zappos customer service rep—I wish I knew her name—talked to me about how the boots felt. The first thing she did was listen. Then she asked a few questions, and again she listened. Soon we were in a real conversation, not a transaction. She reassured me that if I wasn't happy, I could box up the boots and send them back.

Zappos is well known for its willingness to take merchandise back, but here is the difference: telling customers about your return policy is one thing, but having customers experience a genuinely kind and thoughtful person bringing it to life is the difference between disappointed customers and those who rave about you. I kept the boots, and to this day—whenever I wear them—someone inevitably offers a compliment. Zappos doesn't treat you like a traitor when you return goods; they are as nice when you send things back as when you buy them.

The Four Seasons Hotel is well known for great service and beautiful properties. Its location in Atlanta has been the scene of more than one family celebration for my husband and me, our daughters, sons-in-law, and grandchildren. We first took the little kids there when they were four and six years old. The staff couldn't have been nicer. They didn't give a hint of that "Oh darn, they brought little kids!" attitude. So impressed was I that I talk about them in a video on my website.[4]

In the fall of 2016, I was at the Four Seasons in Palm Beach for a meeting, just before Hurricane Matthew hit the Florida coast. The hotel staff could not have handled the situation better—they were attentive without being alarming. The organizer of the meeting—The Thought Leadership

Conference—was Alan Weiss. Alan and a representative from the hotel spoke frequently, and Alan updated the attendees often.

Just before noon on the first day of our meeting, Alan decided that to try to continue with the conference would be fruitless, as we were rather distracted by the hurricane that looked more and more like it was headed our way. Soon after, the hotel announced that the property would be evacuated the next day.

What happened next was terrific. Not the hurricane part. The hotel arranged for transportation to other hotels near the airport, made arrangements for accommodations, and offered to help with flights. If you needed help, they offered it. As you might imagine, an entire hotel emptying out in less than a day created an entirely different situation than is typical. The hotel put on extra staff. The person who checked me out was not dressed in the expected manner, but his attentiveness and knowledge were supreme. My colleagues experienced similarly polite and efficient service in getting out of Dodge—and Matthew's path.

Once home, I realized that I'd left two critical items behind. I called when the hotel reopened and learned that they had both been retrieved and kept safe. They were sent to me promptly. The staff had wrapped my items carefully and enclosed a note saying they were sorry that I had to depart before the planned date.

Boots, Beaches, and a Bank

While the situation with the boots was a mere gray cloud, and a hurricane could be a full-on disaster, the people at Zappos and the Four Seasons have several things in common. First, they focused on what their customers were experiencing. They didn't tell me what to think or feel—they listened.

Before you blow past this observation and tell yourself that your people do this, check it out. Usually, customers experience being "told" but not being heard. You, the leader, must have a better ability to discern the difference. Telling is *not* about helping—*listening* is. You earn the right to share knowledge and information *after* people feel heard, and not a moment before. Otherwise, your advice, platitudes, or expert advice is generic—mere platitudes.

Unfortunately, people in service roles tend to default to reciting rules rather than facilitating solutions. What is on their mind is what they are acknowledged for, rewarded for, and encouraged to do by their supervisors. If the benefits bestowed are contrary to the values, guess what wins?

Look around your own organization and see what's really going on. What decision criteria are you teaching? What decision criteria do you value?

Are your people being guided to tune in or talk? Are they thinking the following?

- What will be most helpful to our customer?
- How can I help customers achieve what they want?
- Is this interaction creating a relationship?
- Am I telling or am I having a conversation?
- Is this person someone I can help?

Discerning the true nature of the exchanges between your employees and your customers is critical. The recently departed CEO of Wells Fargo says he didn't know the nature of the interactions between customers and employees in the bank's retail branches. It turns out that many of these interactions were for the purpose of achieving a short-term gain, but at great long-term cost. I have no doubt that the environment led to much of the fraudulent employee behavior we now know about. An environment, or culture, that condones, encourages, and rewards bad behavior will invariably engender bad behavior—even in people who have good intentions.

The notion that good people will not give in to a bad environment or pressure is untrue. While it may disappoint you to learn it, one of the most studied phenomena in behavioral science is the effect of the environment on behavior. Numerous prominent psychologists, including Stanley Milgram,

Solomon Asch, and Philip Zimbardo, have shown us how susceptible we are to social and environmental pressure to alter our behavior from what we believe is right.

Zappos and the Four Seasons have done a good job of hiring well and creating an environment that not only provides external rewards for doing a good job but also encourages and celebrates the intrinsic rewards in doing so. Pride and a sense of achievement for pro-social and helpful behavior— multiplied by the number of employees you've got—equals huge value. Failure to discern the actual environment and its effect on people's behavior leads to risk, and even crisis.

Courageous Patience

When I talk with leaders about how to proceed in a high-stakes transition, they are often surprised by some of the advice. Indeed, it can seem not only counterintuitive but also wrong. My advice? Pause, think, and decide where to put your focus first. What you do first will be long remembered. What you do first will send a message about your priorities. What you say first will be either enhanced or undermined by how you say it and to whom.

Because good leaders tend to be decisive, they often find it hard, if not unthinkable, to slow down. This is particularly difficult when the risks are subtle and the consequences far off. Unwittingly, a newly appointed leader may focus on what she needs to do while her objectives slowly fade away. This results in the mechanical performance of a series of tasks or events, leading to meager results.

When Drew Madsen became president of Olive Garden restaurants, he had a challenge. Madsen was a marketer, but in a restaurant company, most of the people are in operations. To lead effectively, one must have credibility with people in operations. If you come up through that side of the business, credibility is granted day one—as it was when Dave Pickens succeeded Madsen a few years later. However, if you don't come through that route, you must earn credibility.

When Madsen was named president, he did something that colored his leadership reputation from that day forward. He got on a plane and went all over the country visiting Olive Garden restaurants. Madsen said, "I'm doing a whirlwind tour." My reaction was that this could either be great, or it could be a mechanical exercise. It was the former.

Madsen spoke to everyone he could, and he ate a lot of pasta—and probably more than a few breadsticks. He asked questions and listened to the answers. He displayed curiosity and sincerity. He was not above putting on a vacuum backpack. Somewhere in the corporate office, there may still be a photo of him wearing the vacuum.

In less than two weeks, the phone lines were hot. General managers called each other to talk about Madsen. They were deeply impressed. What was he doing to gain all this positive attention from the people who worked for him out in the field? He was earnest, accessible, and low key. The operators, who were initially skeptical of Madsen's credentials, became enthusiastic fans. Hundreds of general managers with an attitude of optimism are a powerful force. This tidal wave of positive emotion carried the organization forward long enough for Madsen to prove that he was an able leader of this operationally driven company.

Sincerity Is the Great Force Multiplier

If Drew Madsen had ignored the thousands of people who work in Olive Garden restaurants, he would have been viewed through a distant lens—clouded by rightful cynicism. He could have stayed in the corporate office, studying the numbers (he did that too). But he would have made the critical mistake of not allowing others to get to know him, and missed the opportunity to learn. That would have been a big mistake, but it's one that many leaders make—even as they schedule ceremonial visits to "the field." This is often done in the interest of time and in the mistaken belief that the important work happens in the executive suite. It happens everywhere.

Failure to show sincere curiosity says, "I know everything, and you have nothing to tell me." It also tells people on the front lines that the job they do is important, but they aren't. This is not the message you want to send to the thousands of people who look your customers in the eye every day, who speak to them, serve them, and create their view of your company.

Madsen took a risk by putting himself out there to his people in a very vulnerable way, but he gained credibility as a result. Hundreds of people in Olive Garden restaurants felt they got to know him, and they liked his willingness to listen and learn. He showed his desire to learn the most basic things, in public. This was powerful. The credibility it garnered spread to thousands of people throughout the organization, to the people closest to customers.

The investment of a month of travel, listening, asking questions, and connecting with people was a marvelous way to start. Though he didn't plan it, Madsen's actions led to others talking about him in positive terms. This initial positive response, for any leader, gives him credit that makes further positive regard more likely. There is always risk when leaders change, and Madsen reduced that risk by taking the actions he did and doing so with sincerity.

As president, Madsen led the company to quarter after quarter of same-store sales growth before he was named chief operating officer of Darden Restaurants, Olive Garden's corporate parent. He later became president and chief operating officer of Panera Bread.

Lest you think Madsen's behavior was motivated by some scheme or was disingenuous in some way, allow me to disabuse you of that notion. In a recent conversation, I commented on what he had done in his first days on the job as president of one of the largest casual dining restaurant chains in the world. He replied, "What did I do that was so memorable?" The actions he took were out of a sincere desire to learn.

There is no substitute for sincerity, curiosity, and interest in and appreciation for the people who face your customers. This sometimes requires a leader to take a risk or two along the way. But you can't provide shareholder value without understanding the needs of your customers and those whom you wish to become customers—and then responding to them.

Notes

1. Adam Grant, *Originals: How Non-Conformists Move the World.* Viking (2016), p. 57.
2. Wells Fargo, "Our Values," Wells Fargo corporate website, accessed February 15, 2017, www.wellsfargo.com/about/corporate/vision-and-values/our-values.
3. Daniel Kahneman, *Thinking, Fast and Slow.* Farrar, Straus and Giroux (2011), p. 263.
4. CD Consulting Group website, "Vital Marketing Concepts to Grow a Business," www.youtube.com/watch?v=cXT-OxZgEV4.

CHAPTER 7

Brains

When I use the word *brains*, I'm using it in the colloquial way, as in "she's got brains," meaning, she is smart—*intelligent*. Obviously, all humans have brains, but as we also know, people vary widely in intelligence. But beyond raw intelligence, the real question is, what sort of *capabilities* does a given person possess? That is, how well can the person apply her intelligence, skills, and knowledge to achieve her goals—and the goals of her organization? And, finally, how do a person's capabilities affect her judgment?

A lot of research has been done on intelligence and workplace competencies, the recitation of which we could become entangled in, to no good end. Instead, I offer in this chapter a few simple questions to ask yourself that will help you understand your own intellectual abilities *and* more accurately observe the capability of others. Note my use of the plural—*abilities*. Almost every person has areas of intellectual strength that enable good judgment in certain situations; yet we certainly also have other areas where we are less able.

So, how do we measure brains? Is there a reliable assessment that can help us determine a person's native intelligence or, perhaps more important, her capabilities on the job?

To be honest, I am personally not a big fan of assessments. I think they tend to overlook the qualities that make some employees marginal and others great. For example, the Wechsler Scale (IQ) is a well-researched assessment tool that is widely used but not without its limitations. Perhaps the most important thing I learned about this and other tools is there are many distinctions that, while observable, are of little consequence.

Truth be told, we have even more reason to use judgment and discernment when evaluating the intellectual ability of others. The work of Carol Dweck demonstrates that we can increase our intellectual capability, within certain limits.[1] Her research shows that the fixed and unitary understanding of intelligence is incorrect. Rather than send your employees off for full-scale IQ tests, there are more pragmatic ways to gain insight into their brains—and their judgment.

Practical Indicators

The question for leaders is, how can you make useful judgments about the intellectual abilities of others in a way that is pragmatic? To better understand a process that can help, start with yourself. Ask the following:

1. How rapidly do I adapt?
   - What are examples of the times I adapted?
   - How readily will I reconsider a strategy that isn't working?
2. Do I adapt in ways that improve my ability to reach my goals, both objective (such as revenue, margin, customer satisfaction) and subjective (reputation, happiness)?
3. Do I intentionally place myself in situations where I will learn?
   - Do I look at things that are seemingly unrelated to my objectives and look for analogies and metaphors?
4. Am I informed?
   - What am I reading?
   - How much am I reading?
   - Does my reading help me prepare, predict, and pose good questions?
5. When I am learning something new, do I allow myself time to be unsure and to question? Learning requires vulnerability. Snappy retorts do not indicate intelligence or good judgment. Logical inquiry does.

Learning—and doing so intentionally—is a hallmark of people who are bright and successful. Conversely, insularity, unwillingness to adapt, and lack of curiosity do not bode well for those who have adopted those particular traits.

Breathing Your Own Exhaust

When people or companies are insular, they tend to get all their information—and I use that word loosely—from a few sources. They disdain new experiences and new ways of looking at something, and they tend to be more judgmental than curious. In addition, they are much more likely to say *why* things won't work than to ask *how* they might.

I once spoke with a small-company chief financial officer about asset allocation. Just before this meeting, I heard Carol Tomé—the chief financial officer of The Home Depot—speak on the topic. Her remarks stuck with me, and I wanted to share them with this chief financial officer, Kevin. He said, straight-faced, "We aren't The Home Depot." No curiosity, no willingness to see what might be gleaned, no desire to see what could be transferred to his company. This level of defensiveness is antithetical to good judgment.

Insularity leads to rigidity because it constrains your environment and reduces the possibility that things that will provoke you will come into your view. It is the opposite of being educated, regardless of credentials. A person with a PhD in physics can be rigid, though, contrary to the myth perpetuated by the proudly uneducated, it is untrue that highly intelligent and educated people are usually narrow-minded, lack common sense, or are boring. Anyone can be stilted and boring, but the cause isn't education. It is rejection of breadth of knowledge, regardless of how it is acquired, in favor of a superior attitude.

A few years ago, while working on CEO succession with a board, Art—a director—told me, "Liberal arts degrees are worthless." I asked why he thought this was the case. He replied, "Why would anyone spend four years studying art, literature, and mythology?" Art has a technical background and is expert in his field, but he suffers from bounded reality; that is, he believed everything he knows is all there is to know. Art is no less aggressive, judgmental, and bombastic when he doesn't know as when he does.

Later, I asked the chairman why Art was on the board in the first place. The question led this company to reexamine its decision, and he is no longer on the board. Why? He wasn't learning. As the market changed and technology brought new challenges and opportunities, as always happens, he continued to sing the same song and his value crashed.

Banking on the Arts

CEO succession is one process in which insularity and willful ignorance have no place. Selection and oversight of a chief executive officer is the most important role of the board. The CEO runs the company, while the board provides oversight in the interests of the shareholders. A lot can go wrong before a board knows the extent of an issue. Stock price, reputation, customers, suppliers, and partners can all be harmed by a CEO who is either not capable or is blinded by one of the many things that can keep him from seeing what is going on. Selecting a person who is capable isn't enough. The CEO must be a person of integrity and possess great capacity for discernment. Even, and perhaps especially, when things appear to be going well.

Virginia Hepner, a fourth-generation banker from Kansas City, knew she wanted to be in commercial banking from a young age. Growing up, her parents encouraged all four of their children to explore what they were interested in and to "use their talents." She says her parents' message was also "don't be a bystander."

When I spoke with Hepner, I realized that she is not only bright and experienced, but she has three other qualities that have enabled her to perform, lead, and be a role model. She is curious; she has breadth of knowledge, interests, and experience; and she is of great and admirable character. Curiosity can lead people to explore by reading, taking classes, and so forth, but a curiosity that drives one to participate is even better. It embeds the person not only with information, but also changes her through experience. Hepner's parents' advice, "don't be a bystander," was heeded well.

It was obvious during her high school years that she would not only go to college but also that she would head to a very good school. She went to the University of Pennsylvania, where she studied business and art history. While a student, Hepner realized that, unlike her classmates who mostly wanted to get to New York, she preferred to head to the South. After an interview with what was then Wachovia Bank, she bravely told them that she wanted the job and would accept it, if offered.

This approach was successful for Hepner, I think, for a couple of reasons. First, she was open and gave the interviewers information about where she stood. Second, she removed some doubt for them. No one likes to be turned down, even crusty bankers, and no one wants to go through multiple rounds to fill spots if the job can be made simpler. Her willingness to be open and straightforward—as well her astuteness in showing the other party how it would be better off in working with her—are qualities that have benefited Hepner and those around her for many years.

After her retirement from the bank, Hepner was approached by the Woodruff Arts Center in Atlanta—the third largest arts center in the United States. Within the center are the High Museum of Art, Alliance Theatre, and Atlanta Symphony. From its earliest days, the center used what is now commonplace—a shared services model. Providing support to various organizations alleviates the need for duplicate functions, such as finance. The center provides services worth $22 million, which is not allocated to the various arts groups. The 501(c)(3) organization relies on memberships and donors to fund the operation.

As Rachel Moore did when she accepted the role of CEO at the Los Angeles Music Center, Hepner took on the leadership of an organization in financial stress. In fact, arts organizations all over have found it increasingly difficult to raise the money they need. When Hepner took over, the symphony was losing money, the center had issued debt, patrons were asking questions, and then the symphony musicians went on strike. At times like these, boards and patrons often begin to ask detailed questions, and they frequently question the organization's mission. Hepner's statement that there is "no mission without margin" is wonderfully clarifying. Her financial knowledge was crucial at this time but not more important than her disciplined way of thinking and her willingness to follow a logical path—no matter what she discovered along the way.

Hiding in Plain Sight

Not long after Hepner took over, a questionable invoice came to her attention. A recently departed employee had submitted an invoice that he had approved for payment. The accounting department had questions, the head of finance had questions, and ultimately the issue came to Hepner. Her experience as a banker—along with her discipline and candor—led her to do exactly the right things.

First, she was determined to find out what was going on without alerting people that an investigation was taking place. She didn't know the extent of the issue, who knew about it, or who else may have participated. Second, she went to the chairman of the board and told him what she knew, what she didn't know, and what she was doing about it. Third, when more facts were available and it was clear how the situation had arisen, she and the chairman went public with the issue.

Naturally, much criticism was heaped on the institution and on Hepner. While it was no fun, for Hepner there is no option but to tell the truth. It helps that she is so bright and that her experience in business enabled her to be discerning about what she knew and didn't know, and to make the right decisions. Even so, were she strictly a financial person with little appreciation for the arts (remember she studied finance *and* art history), she would have found it easier to deal with the issue in a more transactional way.

The board of trustees, in choosing Virginia Hepner, made a wise decision. Whatever effort they expended to do so, it was worth the cost to get to the right decision about who will lead the organization. After five years at the helm of the Woodruff Arts Center, Hepner announced her retirement. The board and, indeed, the Atlanta community were fortunate to have had

Hepner leading this important institution. The next leader will be wise to listen to her counsel as he or she assumes the role.

Why Smart People Do Stupid Things

Intelligence is highly prized in business, and for good reason. Of course, it is no guarantee of effectiveness, good judgment, or admirable character. Yet, the more able a person is intellectually, the more she can learn and apply what she's learned in novel situations, and the more likely it is that she can even imagine novel situations before they occur.

You may be waiting for me to say, "but . . ." You are right to be waiting, and here it is. Smart people can do stupid things even if they are well intended, empathetic, and adaptable. Why? The human mind is not merely a container of information that stores and retrieves data. It is part of us and, as such, is influenced by our biochemistry, which in turn is influenced by our experiences and our reactions to them.

In short, thinking is influenced by our emotions. Add to this the perceptual and cognitive limitations of our brains, and you begin to understand that it is far more than a data-in, data-out system.

Fortunately, we humans have brains capable of processing information on a literal level, but also to envision, create, and understand metaphor; to predict; and to learn from both direct and indirect experience. We are also lulled into mistakes by our limitations and emotions, including a sense of superiority. This sense of superiority can be a major stumbling block to our success and happiness. A big part of adapting is letting go of what worked in the past, and sometimes our beliefs. The more resistant we are to letting go, the fewer "aha" moments we will have. It's tough when the thing we won't let go of is a superior attitude, because it keeps us from learning—the very thing that enables adaptation. What exactly does this look like?

Overconfidence is perhaps the most common cause of smart people doing dumb things. Research by Paul Schoemaker, Daniel Kahneman, and others is quite clear. We humans are an overconfident species. Leaders should spend no time arguing this, but a lot of time trying to avoid it and interfere with it. A clue? When there is a bandwagon to jump on, be very discerning about whether or not it has real value, or if it is a party on its way to nowhere.

Bounded reality—which I briefly mentioned earlier in this chapter—is another invisible trap. The idea is "everything that I see is all there is." Not only do we get stuck in this way of thinking, but even when we are presented with alternatives, we value what we know from our own experience far more than the expertise of others. This is never more true than when emotions run high. It creates great danger when my experience of something once is over-weighed versus peer-reviewed research results. Your uncle may have survived a hurricane on a barrier island years ago, but that is not evidence that you should ignore a mandatory evacuation. His luck does not constitute a probability or principle, it's just luck.

Anxiety avoidance can also cause smart people to do dumb things. Freud had a lot to say about anxiety, most important that people don't like it and will defend against it—even if the avoidance causes them further discomfort. He was right. Just last week I observed people in a workshop who were asked to role-play giving and receiving feedback. Most people I know in business profess no discomfort with giving or receiving feedback. This is utter nonsense—it is a process fraught with discomfort, leading to much personal and corporate pain because people tend to avoid it.

I learned more about these human foibles when I was a stockbroker than at any other time. Later, in graduate school, and afterward—as the literature in behavioral economics expanded—I learned more. However, some of the most potent memories I have of smart people doing stupid things are from my time as a broker.

A Fool and His Money . . .

During my time as a broker, I realized that many of my clients were utterly convinced that their decisions were wise. I also realized that attempts to persuade them with facts were futile. I needed to find a better way to get people to think about what they were doing. Thus was born my first process visual (see Figure 7.1).

On the line, the poles are defined from least risk to greatest risk. Make a mark on the line corresponding with the risk you are willing to take with your investments.

I showed this visual to my clients, then handed them a pen and asked them to make an X on the line. Then, I explained to them what sort of investments corresponded to the numbers. In this drawing, the number *1* represents Treasury bonds and the number *10* represents uncovered options. Depending upon your own circumstances, you can put different descriptors along the line. A 1 could represent "stay the course," and 10 might represent "change our business model." While this seems simple and perhaps simplistic, a less complex framework often leads to insight. Anyone can complicate. When the stakes are high and good judgment is needed to make important decisions, we don't have time to untangle a complicated model.

It's far better to have people literally place their own mark specifying their preference or assessment of a situation. I had my clients write their initials and the date on these assessments, and I clipped the papers to their client record. This served as a reminder to us about why we made specific decisions.

The professor who said he could tolerate high risk did so because he believed he had found the secret formula for investing. He didn't anticipate how frantic he would get when things went against him. When his investments took a nosedive, he couldn't sell quickly enough. Fear was not in his formula, but it is common for people to sell when investments lose value. Even if we know it isn't a good idea, emotions can dominate our judgment.

Risk Tolerance

Close to Zero   **Could Lose It All**

Figure 7.1 *Risk Tolerance*

Torque, Speed, and Traction (TST™)

Today, when working with clients, I offer them a simple framework or model—often created on the spot. Then I *ask* them how they see their business, using the framework. Specifically, when we are talking about strategy implementation, the following has proven useful (see Figure 7.2):

If you have torque and speed but no traction, you'll spin your wheels. If you have speed and traction but no torque, you'll run off the road. If you have torque and traction without speed, you'll be too slow. But if you have all three, you can steer, control your speed, and keep the wheels on the road. In short, you'll get to where you want to go.

One company that used this model created a dashboard with each aspect defined in more detail and in a way that was relevant for it. The company used it to track and make adjustments as it implemented a new strategy.

The integration of DSC and MFS, first discussed in chapter 1, had torque, speed, and traction. The torque was provided by the leaders and the speed was dictated by their expectations, which varied depending upon

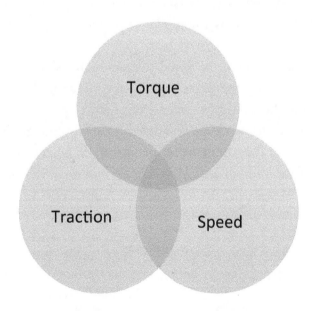

Figure 7.2 *Torque, Speed, and Traction*

where they were in the process. This was an important factor, as speed doesn't just mean "fast," it means the right speed and traction. The traction was greatly increased by setting up a way for the Manheim field leaders to get to know the DSC team. Many were unsure of how this would work out, until it did.

Mergers and Acquisitions Needs More Brains and Fewer Blueprints

If you want to hang out with analytical people who are not scientists, find a group that works in mergers and acquisitions. From financial planning and analysis folks to investment bankers, private equity partners, and more, there is no shortage of experts who have one thing in common: formulas. No doubt, the analysis of a prospective deal is pivotal, and no amount of skillful integration will make a bad deal good. Yet, the emphasis is overwhelmingly on the side of numbers, quantitative analysis, and the search for synergy. Leaders who are new to the game tend to look for a map with the routes identified. What they need is a compass.

When Buffets, Inc. bought the Ryan's Steakhouse chain in 2006, it hired a well-known consulting firm to assist with the integration. The focus was on finance, information technology, human resources, and the like. The process was solid and, looking through a project management lens, it was good. However, this deal had no traction. It was a "good on paper" deal, and investment bankers urged the companies to merge. When I arrived on the scene, Robert Fulghum's book title *It Was on Fire When I Lay Down on It*, came to mind. The company went into bankruptcy less than two years later. Before you skewer the CEO, I'll fill you in. The CEO was, and is, a very good guy who tried to do the right thing, despite the bad decisions of others, who then expected him to create a miracle. He led the company through the bankruptcy and back out again.

The private owners had a good idea. The companies operated in different geographies with little overlap. Their concepts were similar, as was their demographic. The numbers looked right, and the need to weld the pipes of one company to those of another (finance, IT, HR, etc.) is necessary. Once the deal was struck, off they marched. It was a case of very good, skillful procedures being applied to the wrong situation. Unfortunately, the company continued to struggle long after.

Contrast this situation with the Reckitt & Colman and Benckiser situation. The leaders had a very strong purpose (so did Buffets and Ryan's) and a clear plan for integration. What they also had was a realistic assessment of the situation in multiple dimensions. Vision, talent, operations, culture, and financial synergy are the five big categories I find essential.[2] Leave one out and you'll struggle. Leave two out and you'll be doomed.

The Ontology of the Parrot

I heard this phrase often when I was working with Bank of America executives. They used it to refer to people who could repeat words or phrases, but had no grasp of the meaning. When the stakes are high, leaders need to understand their people well enough to discern who has a grasp of the ideas and intent, and who is merely repeating phrases.

In a different company, a division president asked me, "Why do I think people are smarter than you think they are? Am I that bad at reading people?" My answer was, and is: three things masquerade as intellectual ability, and this can fool even experienced leaders.

The proxies are:

- Vocabulary
- Experience
- Knowledge

While vocabulary, experience, and knowledge are useful, they are not the same thing as intelligence. This isn't the place to get deep into the research on intelligence, about which there is much discussion and disagreement among people who spend their professional lives working to understand the topic.

In business, it is critical to know the following about people:

- Do they take in new information with discernment? That is, can they tell the difference between data and information? Do they recognize that one swallow doesn't a summer make? Can they get to the core of an issue, or are they distracted by irrelevant detail? The amount of energy wasted in businesses by people who cannot discern the meaning in data is incalculable. What leads us astray?
  - All I see is all there is, also known as *bounded reality*.
  - Examples close to me are more valid than data from afar.
  - Herd mentality.
- Is their skepticism useful, or is it in service of a superior attitude? People who are self-appointed auditors look for inconsistencies. They like to play "gotcha." These folks are very busy because human beings are inconsistent. Attorneys get paid to do this, and many of them are neither happy nor likable. My attorney, Russell Jones, is a notable exception. Thank you, Russell. It is important to be consistent in matters of ethics, safety, and brand. Otherwise, lighten up!
- Can they extract meaning, see patterns, and generate insights from both quantitative and qualitative information? Observational data are extremely useful to leaders, but it is not as neat as quantitative data. Quantitative is nice, but you need the right data to answer the question you are asking. Too often, we are distracted by the irrelevant.
- Are they willing and able to make decisions, even the tough ones? Ready, aim, fire—or occasionally ready, fire. Ready, ready, ready, aim, aim, aim, aim . . . now the market and your competitors have passed you by.

Overlooked Path to Profit

Leaders will very likely have people around them who are *complicators*—those who tell you how to build a watch when you ask for the time. Trying to get people to change their default approach is difficult but not impossible.

Because people occasionally do change their approach, legions of training and development people are unleashed on organizations, at great cost and for little gain.

My advice? Stop doing that.

Rather than attempting to reshape square pegs, go find the round ones. They are out there. If you consistently hire square pegs when you need round ones, you don't have a selection problem, you have a de-selection problem. The methods you are using are letting too many people through the filter who are not a fit.

Leaders very often tell me that they knew, early on, that someone was not the right person. They could tell right away that this wasn't going to work. So why hang on? Perhaps it is a sense of obligation, embarrassment, or some ridiculous protocol that prevents rapid action. Even smart people allow their powers of discernment and judgment—and their urge to act—to be blunted by emotions.

Let's stop criticizing ourselves and one another for this human condition, and let's not deny that we are emotional creatures. It doesn't improve our judgment to hide from the facts. Let's use that recognition (our brains and cognitive powers) to help people get out of roles that don't fit them any more than they fit the business. This can be done with kindness and support. People don't die from being fired.

Notes

1. Carol Dweck, *Mindset: The New Psychology of Success*. New York: Random House (2006).
2. Constance Dierickx and Linda Henman, "Deal or No Deal," last updated August, 2016, www.cdconsultinggrp.com/wp-content/themes/cdconsult/pdf/Deal-or-No-Deal.pdf.

PART III

Fortitude

Fortitude is the marshal of thought, the armor of the will, and the fort of reason.

—Francis Bacon

CHAPTER 8

Leverage

Courage and judgment are powerful and especially needed in high-stakes situations. Judgment without courage makes for interesting analysis but nothing else. Courage without judgment can motivate action, right or wrong. But, when combined—in the same place and at the same time—courage and judgment help leaders set direction and build enthusiasm to move toward it, leveraging themselves and their organizations many times over.

Necessary as they are, however, they are insufficient to fulfill a strategy. It is the implementation of great ideas that trips up many businesses, organizations, and individuals. My clients often ask, at the beginning of a strategic thinking process (notice I didn't say strategic *planning* process), "How do we make sure this isn't merely an exercise that will sound good but take us nowhere?" Fair question. Sadly, too many leadership groups (notice I didn't say *teams*) come to a discussion about strategic direction with a cynical attitude and perhaps obstructionist intent. I never assume it but have certainly observed it.

What exactly does the top leader need to make use of the courage and judgment she possesses, and that which resides in the company? Fortitude. Without fortitude, little is accomplished. Fortitude provides leverage for those who have it. It is an amplifier for courage and animates judgment.

Fortitude Not Force

When I was doing research about the three-part model of a successful high-stakes leader, I asked people what the words *courage, judgment,* and *fortitude* meant to them. *Fortitude* was the word around which there was the most agreement. My research indicates that for most people, fortitude means strength, determination, and perseverance. Those definitions sound right to me, but are not quite enough.

Fortitude, as I have observed it in the best cases, has an aspect of character. In my conversations with leaders, they often speak about character—that is, having strong character. When I think about the leaders whom I most admire, they not only get great results but also take their organizations to a more solid place in terms of culture and vision. They point toward a purpose that is central to their work—a guiding light.

Cheryl Bachelder, former CEO of Popeyes Louisiana Kitchen speaks about this in her book *Dare to Serve.* When Bachelder became the leader of Popeyes, things were not going well. Fast forward to today. Bachelder oversaw a remarkable turnaround at Popeyes, one admired and touted on national business television shows. She was also recently awarded the Lettie Pate Whitehead Evans Award by OnBoard in Atlanta. OnBoard is an organization whose mission is to increase the number of women on corporate boards and in the executive ranks. *Fortitude* is a word that describes Cheryl Bachelder, OnBoard and, indeed, the woman (the first to serve as a director of a major American corporation) for whom the award is named.

In February 2017, Cheryl Bachelder and Popeyes Louisiana Kitchen announced that the company would be acquired by Burger King. In the time Bachelder was CEO, she took the company from troubled to ripe for acquisition at a price attractive to shareholders.

In CEO transitions, I am constantly struck by the lack of attention given to aspects of character and fit, in favor of pedigree. These things are not mutually exclusive, but rather two sides of the same coin. Overemphasis of one over the other is more than ill advised, it is irresponsible.

A stumbling block for many making decisions about top leaders, not only CEOs, is the difficultly in assessing character, which can be a very subjective thing. Results are far easier to evaluate because quantitative data are available and verifiable. Personal attributes are more challenging, especially in situations where people are trying to present their best face to an interviewer. Not just the candidate but also the hiring company is interested in looking good.

When The Home Depot chose Bob Nardelli as its new CEO in 2000, the company got a GE leader with a ton of experience, but his character was ill suited to the company. His successor, Frank Blake, had also been at GE, but was of a very different character. The results were dramatically different. Bob Nardelli, Frank Blake, and Cheryl Bachelder all have fortitude, but it is expressed differently in each.

To explain why character is so important, I developed the Fortitude Formula after observing hundreds of leaders over more than two decades.

The Fortitude Formula

Vision + Mission + Persistence × Character = Fortitude

Vision is a picture of the future state you desire. It is aspirational. For example, the Partnership Against Domestic Violence (PADV) has as its vision, "A community free of domestic violence."

Mission answers the question, why does your company or organization exist? The mission of the PADV is "To end the crime of intimate partner violence and empower its survivors." This is a bold statement and it's not hard to imagine, given the sad statistics, that the group will not meet the goal in the short term. Yet, that statement drives the board and staff every day and informs decisions large and small.

Persistence is the ability and intention to stay the course. Far from blind ambition, it is a reasoned application of energy and resources. A measure of belief in what one does is needed to have persistence. When I was interviewed for my doctoral program, I was asked what would cause me to drop out. I said, "Nothing. I will finish this program or a similar one elsewhere, but I will, someday, finish my degree." When said with calm assurance, a statement of persistence such as this is powerful.

Character

Why you do what you do, how you do it, and the determination you show are important, but one thing distinguishes greatness—even among those who are successful in all other regards. That is character. What difference are you trying to make with your vision, mission, and persistence? Character is deeply personal.

Jim Kennedy, chairman of Cox Enterprises, says about the continuity of a family-owned business:

> It can't just be about the money. It also has to be about doing good and being a contributor to society. We are extremely proud of our company's products and services, but we're even more proud of programs like the Cox Employee Relief Fund and Cox Conserves. These let us help employees in need, and lessen our impact on the environment. Our family rallies behind this because we want to leave the company and the world in a better place than we found it.

What makes statements such as this credible, are the actions that follow. For this to happen, people need to know about the actions. Robert Cialdini, the leading expert on influence, calls this "giving people access to a laudable trait." Words can call attention to a positive attribute, but evidence that it is real is even better.

Cialdini gave the example of Warren Buffett's letter, which accompanies each Berkshire Hathaway Annual Report. Buffett always mentions losses in the report first. Later, he talks about increases in value. This is important because, as Cialdini says, "It allows you to exhale. You are no longer on guard." When leaders communicate in a forthright manner, it frees us up to listen to what else they have to say. When leaders hide bad news, such as burying it in the fine print of an annual report, the audience is preoccupied by looking for what they fear may be obscured.

Warren Buffet has the fortitude to be open and honest, and reliably so. He earns our trust by what he does. Robert Cialdini says when people are honest, especially when they admit to error, they "establish themselves as an honest source of information. Thus, subsequent information is also deemed credible."

Sisyphus and Archimedes

Inevitably, there are people who, upon reading a word or idea, will think of or give voice to its most rare expression or extreme exaggeration. For example, courage taken to the extreme can lead to recklessness, and extreme judgment can lead us to take note of distinctions that, while real, have no practical significance. Fortitude can also be overdone. Stubbornly adhering to ideas or plans that have little value or are even detrimental—or that have outlived their usefulness—is neither admirable nor valuable. Fortitude needs courage and judgment to be more than brute, relentless force.

Think of Sisyphus from Greek mythology. As punishment for his transgressions against the gods, Zeus condemned Sisyphus to push a boulder up a steep hill, only to have it roll back down to the bottom again—repeating without end. Richard Taylor, the philosopher, interprets the myth as a metaphor for the lack of meaning in mindless repetition.[1] In the myth, Sisyphus's task was not one he chose (conscious) nor one he acquired by habit (unconscious). It was a sentence for his bad behavior.

Surely, no one reading this would deliberately set up such meaningless tasks in the belief they would get the rock up the hill or their strategy to fruition. Yet, organizations have meaningless practices and habits that suck the life out of those who must adhere to them or see that others do.

The overuse of fortitude, determination, and drive create an environment in which changing a practice is regarded with suspicion, even as traitorous. The metaphors of force are familiar to most. For example, "His people would run through a wall for him," is said with pride about a leader who inspires intense loyalty. In such an environment, reactions to change can be strong, emotional, and even fanatical. Rigid, ossified cultures are barriers to implementing strategic shifts. It can take the organizational equivalent of breaking bones to reset them. It isn't easy, and pain is certain.

Leverage

As an alternative to mindless repetition and meaningless tasks, embrace the idea of leverage. Archimedes, a mathematician who lived in the third century BC, said, "Give me a place to stand, and I shall move the Earth." Though Sisyphus had no option but to push the rock with his own force, Archimedes used reason to describe the nature and power of levers. A lever creates power by using a plank and force around a fulcrum.

Think about a teeter-totter. Children quickly figure out how to use this playground equipment and enjoy it without knowing the names of concepts such as fulcrum, lever, force, weight, and momentum. Kids experiment with force and momentum by:

- Altering where they sit—close to the middle, at the far end, or anyplace in between.
- Changing the force used when sitting—gingerly or aggressively.
- Adding friends.
- Removing friends.

Great leaders alter where they sit, how much force they use, and who they have with them, but have more awareness of the likely consequences of their decisions. They also observe—they aren't always on the plank. But, to the point Archimedes made about a place to stand, leaders need to ask, "Where do I need to stand?" as well as, "What do I stand for?"

It's obvious that you can generate more influence by adding people to one or the other end of the lever. Layers of management and complex procedures add weight. Added weight prevents wild swings on the other end, yet it also reduces power. Too little weight, and you are buffeted about and even tossed to the ground.

Some leaders unwittingly use their influence to create stability. To prevent wild swings and avoid getting injured, they seek a steady state. This is not the goal. The goal is to generate value. Companies that choose stability over dynamic balance set themselves up for extinction. Eastman Kodak, Borders, and Circuit City are examples of companies that didn't adapt, and that failed as a result. Recently, some retail merchants have blamed a lack of popularity of shopping malls for their bad results—this while others, in those same malls, grow and succeed. Blaming "the market" merely justifies the status quo, but there is no leverage in that.

Those who don't act may have a good process for gathering information, organizing, and reviewing it. In the extreme, this is navel gazing. Customers are not moved by your insights or pronouncements. If you serve them well, they may not even realize what insights you have or what it took to get them. The teeter-totter doesn't move when things are in perfect equilibrium, and money doesn't make money—the movement of money creates value, and insights alone provide no leverage.

The same is true for employees: the best want to achieve something. Align your service with customer needs and watch what happens. Match employees' talents and interests with your needs and the same is true. Now, give them autonomy to achieve, and the wheels will really start to turn!

An Uncomplicated View of Change

The persistence with which people generate complicated models is fascinating. Somewhere along the way, many got the message that the more complex the model and the more slides in a deck, the smarter you look. This is utter nonsense. Complicating may justify the foolish way firms charge for their services (billable hours) and probably soothes those who insist that their business is "different, unique, special." What complexity doesn't do is create clear, powerful, and memorable stories that help us get on the right track and stay there.

A couple of years ago, a client handed me a huge presentation from a well-known consulting firm. Their bill for the presentation was a cool $2 million. The first two slides of the presentation told the story, admittedly in multisyllabic words, but it was a solid idea. The rest was proof. Perhaps the leaders needed the proof, but I don't think so. They are experts in their industry and had advanced this idea on their own. The consultants, specialists in strategy, didn't do anything strategic. They did a ton of analysis. Now, I didn't say that analysis isn't valuable. What I do believe is that more analysis is done under the banner of "strategy" than actual strategic thinking, and that more analysis is done than is necessary.

The same can be said for change. Change comes down to what people do. What do they say, what behavior do they display, and what do they not do? Change management as practiced in most instances is nothing more than communication and training. This is fine, but insufficient, and the reason that many attempts to make changes fall flat. Like the disappointing results from mergers and acquisitions, change efforts leave a lot of money on the table. Here's why: a lack of fortitude causing low leverage.

Robert Cialdini advises that organizations make people aware of the idea of change before announcing a specific change. Statements from leaders leverage what he calls authority to prepare people for change. For example, the use of adages such as "When we are through changing, we are through" influences the mind-set of those who hear it. While adages and sayings are usually difficult to disagree with, they are far from useless. They impact our mind-set and subsequent behavior. Once we agree with a statement, we are loath to engage in behavior that makes us appear inconsistent. Otherwise, cognitive dissonance is ignited. Most of us prefer to avoid or quickly eliminate this uncomfortable state.

The Pivot Point Is You

Psychology has much to tell us about behavior change, some of it from a clinical point of view. Businesspeople tend to reject the work that has been done in clinical settings, believing it doesn't apply to them or their situation. This is false. The human beings who work in companies and organizations are not genetically different from those who are patients in a clinic or hospital. Homo sapiens everywhere and in every circumstance have much in common, regardless of other factors.

When I was involved in a large-scale change effort with a client in the insurance industry, I taught them a very simple, four-part model. The first three parts address the behavior of individuals and offer them an opportunity.

1. What?—What is the change?
2. How?—How will I learn a new way of doing my work?
3. Why me?—How do I fit in? How will I grow, what opportunity will I have? Why am I the right person to be in the new environment? Why are we doing this, anyway?

I didn't make up these categories. They come from very good research on behavior change.[2] I have applied the same concepts in other situations, as have professional colleagues. Elizabeth Gibson, a consultant, led a major change initiative at Best Buy in the early 2000s using the exact framework, resulting in a rise in stock price of more than 1,000 percent.[3]

The third piece is what is often left out of major change initiatives. Companies tell and teach, tell and teach, tell and teach—and nothing much happens. This is because they skip over motivation, give it short shrift, or they try to "motivate" instead of match.

Motivating others is tough stuff, as I'm sure anyone reading this can attest. My advice to my clients is: don't try to create motivation, uncover it. How do you do this?

Know thy people.

You must know the people working with you—*really* know them—if you are going to be able to detect what motivates them, and what shuts them down. No need to panic, this doesn't involve anything personal or untoward. What it does involve is observation and conversation. What do they do well? What do they seem to enjoy doing? What aspect of the work elicits enthusiastic behavior when they talk about it? Those things are a good start.

The motivational aspect of change is the most difficult and, therefore, the one most often skipped. It's a huge miss because when you have people who *want* to do what the business needs, it is far easier to teach them all sorts of new information and skills. Without intrinsic motivation, it's an uphill battle—like the one Sisyphus wages—an energy drain. When motivation is discovered and engaged, it generates energy. And energy is something every organization could use more of.

The Fourth Dimension

When I was a resident at the Medical College of Georgia, we did a lot of work in what is known as behavioral medicine. This unit exists because it is well understood that prescribing medication, rehabilitation, diet, or a routine for self-care is no guarantee that patients will actually do what their doctors recommended. My colleagues and I worked with a wide range of patients and spent a great deal of time on behavior change.

One memorable patient was a teenage girl with type 1 diabetes. Ellen was not consistent about monitoring her diet, checking her blood sugar, or injecting insulin in the proper dose or at the right time. This led to her often winding up in the intensive care unit—one year, she was there seventeen times. We put our heads together to see what we could figure out. Ellen was a smart girl, vivacious and fun. Once she was out of crisis in the hospital, she was a model patient—doing exactly what she needed to do for her own health. So, why did Ellen keep ending up in the hospital? The mystery unraveled when we met her mother. I'll spare you the details and cut to the chase. The environment this girl lived in, outside of the hospital, was bad enough that she was willing to make herself sick—even risk her life—to be away from home.

The fourth dimension in the behavior change model is *context*. Miss this one, and your ability to effect change will be seriously diminished. You may achieve some leverage by informing, teaching, and matching motivation to role, but if the environment does not support the change, it will come to naught. We didn't detect the nature of Ellen's environment until we had a meeting with her mother . . . finally! In organizations, the environment is powerful but not always easy to describe for those in the midst of it. Nonetheless, it is a major determinant of behavior.

Immunotherapy

The model of change I've shown you has four aspects, but they are in two dimensions. This is important to understand because you can do everything in the first three aspects and nothing in the fourth and be left wondering what the heck happened. This is why culture is so important. It is powerful. It will chew up and spit out your strategy, plans, and initiatives very quickly if they conflict with the culture. If your strategy and culture are in conflict, the culture will almost always win. There are probably exceptions to this, but I've never seen them.

One company I worked with embarked on an ambitious set of changes in a short period. First, a new CEO—David—took over the organization. Second, the company shifted its strategy from product focus to market focus, necessitating a redo of marketing, sales, and customer service and an overall mind-set change throughout the company. Finally, the company made an acquisition. Before the acquisition, it had already had many struggles with employees who were resisting the new strategy. The leaders understood it and were completely on board. Others? Some yes, some no. The naysayers were very, very loud. Some were disruptive, and a few were actively undermining it. They made personal attacks against David, accused him of all manner of things, none of which I found any reason to believe.

Here's what the leaders did in this high-stakes situation:

First, they defined the future of the company as a market-facing organization. This meant letting go of the company's long tradition of developing, refining, and selling products.

Second, the chief operating officer laid out the organizational structure they needed. He was very skilled at this, and his reasoning was solid. I took particular note of the rigor he brought to the process and his willingness to be bold in his recommendations. The other leaders agreed with almost all of it. So far, so good.

Third, David and the other senior leaders laid out criteria for each role. Every single role had a good description of what was to be done and how it would contribute to the overall strategic goal.

Fourth, they created a description of behaviors and attributes needed to ensure the strategy would be fulfilled. This addressed behavior such as "willingly listens to opposing ideas."

Finally, people were matched to roles. The process we laid out was this: first the leaders gave an opinion, and then the manager had a conversation with the person about what he or she wanted. There were a few interesting surprises. A couple of people suggested changes for themselves, and one woman—Angela—came to the meeting with an idea that she had fleshed out very well. She landed in a job that was not only new for her, but new to the company. Last I saw her, she was absolutely thrilled—as were the leaders.

The results? Eighteen months later, sales were in record territory, margins were healthy, the company's reputation had improved, and the organization was making investments in employees at an astonishing level. This was a recipe for success, but there were some stumbles along the way. I'll share those here, which is why I chose not to name this organization. The point isn't that the leaders made mistakes. The point is, mistakes are inevitable, but you can't allow those mistakes to erode fortitude if you want to see your plans through.

Nonfatal Missteps

The new CEO talked a big game but equivocated on the five-yard line. Just when you thought he was heading for the end zone, he would stop and question the direction, the play, the ball, the team, and anything else he could think of. This left people confused—most notably his direct reports. As a consultant to him, I was obligated to say, "Just when you look committed to a direction, you pull back. At that point, you tell me and your team that action isn't required, things are better. What is causing you to change course?" This was a pivotal conversation because he recognized his ninety-ninth–hour reticence and the way it impacted others. He was then able to push through it.

The number of people who were deemed a poor fit—but who hadn't been given support or good feedback—was significant. This caused the leaders to question themselves on the grounds of fairness. How could they remove someone who had worked under a lousy boss, had little to no accurate feedback, and had received no encouragement? They ultimately decided to leave a few people in place who fit this description—some worked out, and some didn't. The amount of energy put into this effort was huge, and it was messy and awkward. The employees who were finally given the feedback they needed had to work very hard to catch up. They had to redeem themselves with the leaders and their peers.

A few people who were actively undermining the new strategy were not actively managed. The leaders took too long to address destructive behaviors, though eventually they did. In each case, the issues were more profound than they knew.

The nonfatal but problematic missteps in this organization are common. The error rate will never be zero. However, there are a few points of leverage that are diminished by the mistakes identified here. One is the ability to influence. The CEO in this example diminished his authority by equivocating. This undermined his influence for no good reason. He was neither pursuing a self-serving agenda nor doing anything wrong from a business or ethical point of view. He was anxious. This led him to waver. When stakes are high, the leader needs to be authoritative.

Another principle illuminated here also involves emotion—this time, guilt. Feeling responsible for the lack of guidance, development, and feedback led this leadership team to retain people they would otherwise have let go. They overdid it, however, as is often the case. Some of the people in this group worked out, but most did not. Leaders need to ask themselves in whose interest is their largesse?

By far the biggest error in this case was in not quickly removing those who actively opposed the new leader and strategy. The leaders erred on the side of hope. Their fortitude was worn out and replaced by hope that these folks could be influenced by the leaders and their peers to get on board. While this is understandable, it is usually a pipe dream. Why? Because once we commit to a belief or course of action, it is extremely difficult to change. Human beings are far more likely to justify, rationalize, and explain away inconsistencies than they are to admit that they changed their minds.

The Fortitude to Be Inconsistent

Despite repeated demonstrations that humans are inconsistent, capable of great irrationality, driven by emotion, and have a strong need to rationalize, we continue to be shocked when behaviors indicate our innate humanness. Some spend their careers doing what I call verbal audits. They will help you remember what you said, and gleefully point out any distinctions from what you are saying now. Needless to say, this puts most people on the defense, which raises anxiety and leads to all manner of behaviors to reduce it.

This is normal—rationalization is a protective device. The antidote is a climate where it is okay to change our minds, admit we were mistaken, respond to new information and inputs, and so forth. Sticking to our story line to avoid the sting of criticism that we are "inconsistent" is as limiting as it is to have no opinion at all. It neutralizes the leverage we can gain from change.

Creating an environment where a stake in the ground can be moved takes guts on the part of leaders, but it is essential to leveraging the power of our people and our organizations. We have come to admire consistency in a way that is foolish. When commitment to a consistent methodology blinds us to outcomes, then we are irrationally consistent. Yet, the tendency to defend what we do, even in the face of evidence that it is not effective, is powerful.

Last year, during a strategic discussion, I suggested that the risk-management aspect of a client company's business could improve if the company systematized and documented some of what the leaders referred to as "gut feel." This company, in the finance industry, runs on metrics. It is very profitable and great at what it does. Yet, the leading indicator about whether or not a client's risk profile was changing was referred to in this company as "gut feel." The ability of some people in the company to use observational data and make predictions based upon it was extraordinary, but it wasn't magic. Rather, it was pattern recognition. The most experienced people had learned to mine observational data to make predictions about clients and prospective clients.

The issue was the company was overly reliant on the experience of a few key people who had developed terrific pattern recognition. Yet, the company had a hard time teaching it because most of it was unconscious. It chalked it up to "time in the saddle." Yet, the rate of growth was about to outstrip the small pool of people who possessed this valuable characteristic. Those who were less experienced but very able were not going to get as much experience as their bosses before they had to make some tough decisions.

I suggested that it operationalize what the very experienced people were doing so it could be taught to others—leveraging this organizational strength. This would allow less experienced people to rely on a system that was objective and rational, but drew on a different type of data.

Sam, an executive in the group fired back, at high volume, saying, "We removed all the emotion from our models years ago!" Interesting that he was so emotional about it. Sam was, quite rightly, proud of the work they had done to establish procedures and measures for many important aspects of their business. However, he wasn't seeing that the experience and gut feel the more effective members of the team possessed could be leveraged in a way that is systematic, even if it was not objective by his standards.

In the face of rapid growth, this company had to find a way to transmit methods and skills to a larger group of new employees than at any time in the past. At the same time, the company realized that what had made it successful was the ability of its most successful people to spot subtle indications of increased risk.

The leader was facing a high-stakes situation. The company and its owners were counting on rapid growth but not at the expense of profit erosion due to increased losses. He knew they needed to do something different to help newer employees develop these skills quickly. Yet, this was a culture that valued consistency with near fervor. To make a change, he needed more than the force of his decision. He needed leverage.

Rather than focus on the method, the CEO focused attention on outcomes. He asked, What is the best way to teach our new employees so that we continue to grow without higher losses? This had broad appeal because these measures, revenue, and losses affected everyone. He gained leverage by changing the focus to outcomes first and methods second. Had he allowed the pull of tradition and the drive to be consistent to sway him, he would have gained approval but lost leverage.

Notes

1. Richard Taylor, "Time and Life's Meaning," *Review of Metaphysics* 40 (1987): 675–686.
2. Constance Dierickx, *The Efficacy of a Culturally Tailored Intervention for HIV Prevention in Deaf Adults*. 1998. Doctoral Dissertation.

    J. D. Fisher and W. A. Fisher. "Changing AIDS-Risk Behavior," *Psychological Bulletin* 111 (1992): 455–474.
3. Elizabeth Gibson and Andy Billings, *Big Change at Best Buy*. Nicholas Brealey Publishing (2003).

CHAPTER 9

The Process of Discipline

The word *discipline* is both a noun and a verb. *To discipline* is to teach, train, and correct wrong behaviors. *A discipline* is an area of knowledge, such as the discipline of anthropology, physics, or the law. Discipline for leaders has more to do with disciplined process—it is a necessary aspect of fortitude. Without disciplined process, fortitude may veer into force. With disciplined process, fortitude is better calibrated and becomes an instrument of progress in ways that are precisely what is needed in the circumstance.

Why is this distinction important? First, when we think of discipline, we usually think of an act of will, of staying the course. Often, it is thought to involve effort—even struggle—to control others or our own behavior. Remember Sisyphus? He had fortitude, yes. Disciplined process? No. Of course, in the myth, he had no choice. But we do. Yet, even leaders with much authority make the mistake of thinking they can skip over establishing a process and go straight to tactics. Quickly, and often without awareness, tactics drive decisions. Something may be done very well, but if it is the *wrong* thing that is done very well, it's no good.

In acquisitions or mergers, a rigid plan for integration may be perfectly executed and still fail to yield the desired result. Indeed, the failure rate of deals (estimated to be between 70 percent and 90 percent)[1] suggests that at least part of the issue is a lack of fortitude—or replacing it with force. A lack of discipline about the process of making pivotal decisions leads to mistakes that undermine the investment thesis. Bad decisions—or no decisions—are common without a clear framework. A disciplined process, grounded in the investment thesis, is neither generic nor a planning quagmire. It is what is needed and, often, skipped.

In a recent article in *McKinsey Quarterly* about mergers and acquisitions, the authors Scott A. Christofferson, Robert S. McNish, and Diane L. Sias reported characteristics and practices associated with greater success in capturing the elusive and, some would argue, mythical synergies.[2] The long and short of the article is this: the more deals a company does, and the better its evaluation process and tactics during integration, the better the results. The article details some specifics: for example, better analysis, guarding against overconfidence (the leading cause of deal failures), and doing post-deal evaluations.

This advice isn't bad, but neither is it insightful. Adopting the advice and doing so in a disciplined manner is still suboptimal. Why? It is still a set of tactics. Advising companies to adopt procedures doesn't change what is most fundamental to achieving better results. That is for leaders to have the fortitude to use a disciplined process which, in turn, guides decisions about what to do and when. The article suggests postmortems, which can be a good way to learn.

Here is the distinction: conducting a postmortem is an activity, not an outcome. As such, findings are far more likely to be overgeneralized as recent events loom large in the human mind, and have a powerful effect on the way we see the next event. A leader who has the fortitude to focus on process over methodology, tactics, or habits is more likely to think about which tools are needed in a given circumstance before someone grabs the hammer that worked so well last time.

The Power of No

A company in the finance industry sold to a competitor, and before anyone could even think about what to do—never mind how or when—a large consulting firm showed up on the doorstep of the acquired company.

I happened to meet the team leader from this firm soon after he arrived. The leader and his colleagues set about their work, which involved meeting with each functional leader and explaining what was to happen for the integration.

Problem number one—the consultants were driven by the wrong agenda. They weren't consulting. They were contractors with the word *consultant* printed on their business cards. This is more often than not the case. Have hammer, look for nails.

Second, the leaders of the acquired company hadn't been consulted or included in the planning. Thus, the firm's plans were based on assumptions and not information.

Third, the leaders of the acquired company resented any outsiders—period. They took no time to get to know the leaders or form relationships with them. Their understanding of fortitude was "to be forceful."

The leader of the integration—who had been consulted only in a cursory manner—took stock of this, asked a few questions, and summarily removed the consultants, save one who remained in a project management role. What he was saying no to wasn't so much the individuals, but rather the process by which they appeared on the scene and what they did, or rather did not do, once they arrived.

This is an example of a disciplined process taking priority over the objectives. This is exactly why you can't let the technicians chart the course. They are using a microscope when a telescope is needed. The purveyors of tactics will never be the ones to say no to their own methodology. It takes a leader with fortitude to resist that, and it is never more important than when the stakes are high.

The Hunt for Deals

Looking for a company to acquire and planning the "deal" can be thrilling. You look, you find, you conquer. Hopefully, there is a reasoned thought process about the merits of a union. Whether or not there is, the experience can be a heady one. Dinners, talk about what could be, compliments on your wonderful company—all create an atmosphere of heightened optimism. This can plant the seeds of a poisonous plant that is, nonetheless, quite beautiful: overconfidence.

If you are on the receiving end of this courting, it can be deliciously disorienting. Most of us understand the concept of being blinded by infatuation, but few see the real influence it has on our thinking. The pursuer, seeing signs of encouragement, becomes even more determined to seal the deal. Tension rises and some resolution is needed for it to subside. This is intensified by overconfidence. This deal will work! I'll make it work because I'm smarter than those other guys.

The Rational Dealmaker

At this point, you are probably asking yourself why it is that I'm making smart, successful, rational people sound like jungle animals. Because we humans are far more than brains—we are also highly emotional creatures whose thinking is influenced by amorphous, but powerful, feelings. Our "gut instincts" affect our decisions far more than we care to realize. Indeed, many of you reading this will say, "I am not like that. I am rational." I ask you right now to think about how you *feel* reading that you are not an entirely rational being. Irritated? Smug? That's emotion.

Businesspeople—at least the successful ones—are often described as having drive. This drive may look like energy, passion, even heat. Think about the contestants on the TV show *The Apprentice*. Drive and ambition are viewed as positive attributes, and a lack of either gets people fired fast. That said, loss of control is not regarded positively. Passion is good—being overwhelmed is not.

So why do contestants on *The Apprentice* sometimes show strong emotion, even though they know that losing control will not put them in a positive light? They are human. Even when the stakes are high, indeed especially when the stakes are high, emotion affects what we do.

Not-So-Innocent Bystanders

Let's add to the merger mix people who get paid if your deal goes through—investment bankers or other interested parties who may be compensated only when a deal is done. If the merger later goes south, don't expect a refund. You are aware of this compensation, but the bankers also bring a lot of data and analysis—exactly the sort of stuff that is tailor made to quell your fears. Your confidence goes up because you feel you are being both rational and passionate.

What about the bride or groom telling his or her best friend, wedding planner, parents, or florist, "I'm really not sure about this." Is it cold feet, or a clue that something isn't right? A lot of money has already been spent to throw this shindig. The decision to pull the plug or go ahead is affected by the human tendency to see money spent as a waste if a deal is not fulfilled. This notion of sunk costs (which can be tangible or intangible) leads many a person to stay on an ill-advised course that an outsider would avoid altogether.

Whether your merger is corporate or personal, you will quickly begin to see the wisdom of your decision. There are always surprises, even without misrepresentation. Billions of dollars wasted—and untold agony—result from trying to fix bad decisions. Why not spend a little more time on prevention? The return on investment is far greater.

Five Questions for Disaster Avoidance

While we can't always avoid the negative consequences of forging ahead with an ill-advised merger or acquisition, by asking these five questions we may be able to avoid initiating it in the first place:

1. What do you know about the company you are considering buying or merging with?
2. With reference to the first question, how do you know these things? Where did this information come from?

3. What do you know about the people who interact with the target company? Customers, suppliers, employees, creditors?

4. What does the other party want out of this deal? I'm not talking about what they told you, rather what does your own research say?

5. How easy or difficult has it been to discuss the merger? A bad prospect makes a bad client. A difficult fiancé makes a challenging spouse. People don't magically change once the rings are exchanged or the check has been cashed.

If you plan to grow your business through acquisitions, you would be wise to recognize that the difference between failure and stunning success is not solely related to the quality of your financial analysis. It lies in your ability to manage yourself through the decision-making process and the transition period. This may be counterintuitive but so is swimming parallel to the shore when caught in a riptide. While doing this isn't obvious or natural, it is the best way to keep from drowning. It takes fortitude.

Who Will Lead?

Schnabel Engineering is a firm of consulting engineers who are experts in dealing with the world's most challenging engineering problems. They know more about the interaction of land and water with structures than anyone. How do I know this? Their clients told me. When interviewing clients for them, I heard the following, "If you want to do something and an engineering firm says it can't be done, ask Schnabel. If Schnabel says it can't be done, then you know it can't be done."

Schnabel is a firm of very able engineers, geologists, and experts in risk and hydrology. Sixteen years ago, Schnabel had a change of leadership that was rather sudden. Gordon Matheson, PhD, became the CEO, and immediately upon assuming the role he learned that the company was in trouble. What happened subsequently is a testament to fortitude. Gordon pulled the company back from a very shaky future and led it to growth over the next fifteen years. The firm built its capacity and reputation in a way that others—even its competitors—justifiably admire.

Fifteen years is quite a long time for a CEO to lead. Fortunately, during this time several people in the company had grown into good leaders themselves. A CEO transition is one of the most significant and high-stakes circumstances an organization faces, and is one of the top responsibilities of a board. In the words of Richard Anderson, retired CEO of Delta Airlines, "If you don't have a successor ready, you've failed." Schnabel was ready.

As in most CEO succession processes, those who make the decision typically jump to the question of who? Whom to choose as successor is often regarded as the question, but it is the wrong one. Whom do we need for *what*, is the right question. The right leader depends upon what the organization needs at the time and for the chosen strategy. Yet, jumping to the answer is a natural and understandable impulse. This is why creating a process and implementing it with discipline is so powerful. It is an antidote to leaping to a conclusion.

Power of Process

What did Schnabel do when it came time to begin the search for the company's next CEO? Several things. First, it appointed a committee to oversee the selection process. This is important because the committee was not appointed to choose. Rather, they were asked to come to the board with a recommendation. The board members would make the decision, as they should.

The committee developed and recommended a profile for the next CEO. The profile was grounded in the strategic opportunities and included the attributes and behaviors needed in the new leader, as well as past accomplishments. Too often, in CEO succession, the pedigree overshadows everything else. When Bob Nardelli went to The Home Depot, he didn't lack a strong reputation and track record, but he wasn't successful. Why not? His particular set of attributes didn't allow him to adjust to the company's unique culture. This is a critical aspect of leadership in high-stakes situations, and what Peter Drucker referred to as "self-management."

Each CEO candidate went through an evaluation, based on the profile, which the board had reviewed and approved. These evaluations were done strictly in line with the criteria. They were not reviews of personality, which is not predictive of performance. This is an area of weakness in some high-stakes transitions, when a company places too much faith in highly instrumental methods. Why? Because the evaluation tools and methods are developed in a particular context that is not an exact replica of the situation in which a leader must function. Individual characteristics—as powerful as they are in determining behavior—are far from the *only* determinant.

Leaping to "the answer" can work, but that doesn't make it a good idea any more than planning to earn a living by waiting for the phone to ring because it happened once or twice. When Schnabel was preparing for the retirement of its longtime CEO, Gordon Matheson, the company was very conscious of how well he had served them. Simultaneously, they realized that the future of the firm was going to be different. They were disciplined about how they created the profile for the CEO who would serve *in the future*. This is no easy task. Most often, companies do one of two things, either they look for someone quite like the current leader *or* they look for someone who isn't like the current leader.

Schnabel had laid out a process to guide them through the CEO transition. Again and again, when they had questions, they returned to it. They reminded themselves that the process they created was one they believed would help them make a good decision. Ultimately, the board selected Walter Rabe as president and CEO. In his first year, he led the firm in developing a new strategy and promoted several talented people to help ensure its implementation. The changes have all been made with two things in mind: first, they are building on a strong foundation, and second, the future will not look like the past.

Life-Saving Fortitude

The work of the engineers, geologists, and other professionals at Schnabel may not seem like life and death, but it is. Walter Rabe and his colleagues know very well that when structures fail, either partially or fully, people can be injured or die. They take this responsibility very seriously.

I'm often struck by the courage and fortitude of those whose work improves our lives and, sometimes, saves them: firefighters who run into burning buildings—not with wild abandon, but using judgment that comes from training and experience; and police officers, such as those in my town of Smyrna, Georgia, who recently found and controlled a disturbed person who was on the loose with guns, firing randomly. Officers found the man and took him into custody without anyone being harmed. It takes fortitude, not force, to do this.

The work of some leaders involves saving the lives of those threatened by domestic violence. Nancy Friauf, the president and chief executive officer of the PADV in Atlanta, Georgia, has worked on this issue for decades. PADV is the largest organization of its type in Georgia, and, sadly, the need for the care and services it provides appears endless.

The rate of domestic violence has not changed appreciably in the United States in years. If Friauf and her team were to look to incidence as a measure of their success, they could be discouraged. While they do pay attention to the rate of domestic violence, they look to the individuals whom the organization serves to determine how well they are doing. Friauf says, "You have to look at the big picture and the small picture. Because what we do is so difficult, we must celebrate the small successes while still working on the vast problem of domestic violence and helping survivors."

2017 will be the fortieth year of operation for PADV. While proud of what they have done, Nancy Friauf and her team are acutely aware that tomorrow will bring more people fleeing and, sometimes, people returning to live with the person from whom they were fleeing not long ago. Yet, Friauf, her team, and the board members of PADV must keep working to raise money, run the shelters, and help women get back on their feet with a new place to live, a job, and a feeling of safety.

How does an organization keep going when the need is so great and continues year after year? Friauf speaks about the importance of keeping the mission—"To end the crime of intimate partner violence and empower its survivors"—top of mind while doing the tactical things, day to day, that help individuals. It is a parallel process, one that looks long term at an aspirational goal, and the other very immediate. Friauf and her team must keep both in mind, continuously.

How does Friauf do this? She pays attention to the full spectrum of constituents and stakeholders all the time. Meeting with large donors; visiting the staff running the shelters; working with the board; speaking with local, state, and federal agencies that provide support and require accountability; and maintaining relationships with police, the court system, and attorneys who volunteer to help. Each relationship has its own characteristics, and each constituency its own agenda. One way of relating just won't do.

I found in Friauf some interesting similarities with other leaders, some of whom run very large public companies. They are:

- **A commitment to and enthusiasm for the mission of their respective organizations.** Leaders who are grounded in the raison d'être of their organization provide a model for others and will attract people who share in it. The way the leader conveys her commitment and enthusiasm can vary widely, and it does. Frank Blake left no doubt about his devotion to The Home Depot—nor does Nancy Friauf—but you wouldn't describe their style of communicating in the same way.
- **An open style.** Friauf is relaxed in conversation with people of many types, but is always intentional and earnest. Questions about what PADV is doing, planning to do, or has done in the past receive a response that is decidedly non-cagey. Joe Lee, former chairman and CEO of Darden Restaurants, when asked questions he didn't want to answer, would say—with genuinely good humor—that he couldn't answer because doing so might risk a competitive advantage.

- **Character.** Leaders like Friauf leave no doubt about their agenda, and this leads others to trust them. This strength of character makes a leader stand like a rock on matters of principle and ethics, and to be honest about mistakes.
- **Use of a variety of data.** Top leaders must, of course, understand the numbers and make decisions that lead to financial health. As Virginia Hepner of Woodruff Arts Center says, "There is no mission without margin." Yet, the numbers don't speak in story form. Leaders need the story to inspire and fuel themselves and others. When Friauf, a staff member, or board member asks for support, they know that showing the difference the help will make is critical. Donors want to know what good their donation will do.

Uplifting Fortitude

OnBoard is an organization whose mission is to increase the number of women in executive leadership and on corporate boards. OnBoard was one of the first organizations in the United States to see that achieving its mission would require an organized effort. Further, the organization's leadership knew that they couldn't be effective unless men also understood why the mission is important and were willing to speak publicly about it.

In 1993, OnBoard began reporting on the number of women on corporate boards in Georgia. This was an important step in achieving its mission. You need to know your starting point to know how far you've come, after all. A study has been published annually since then, attracting attention from women, men, and leaders of all types of organizations.[3] Sarah Ernst, president of OnBoard, reminds us that in 1993, only 27 percent of companies based in Georgia had a woman on their board. The number today is 60 percent.

Over the years, OnBoard has kept an eye squarely on its vision, but has made significant changes in *how* it works. Today, men are not only members of OnBoard, but also there are four men on the board—each of whom is vocal about why increasing the number of women in leadership roles and on corporate boards is good for business.

Today, it is far easier to get a male senior executive to speak about the importance of diversity in organizations, at all levels. This is important because people are more influenced by those who are like them than by those who are different in ways that are quickly identifiable (gender, for example).

OnBoard has, over the years, sought out senior executive men and women to speak about the importance of opening one's eyes to the talent in front of them. Psychological research is clear that we can fail to see our own blinders. Rather than accuse those with blinders on, as though they are intentionally blind, it is easier to influence by showing the benefits of recognizing and removing them yourself.

Sometimes You Need Guts

While it is important to influence those who select, promote, mentor, and champion talented people not to overlook women—or any talented individual, for that matter—there is another side of the equation. That is, are the people who want to be selected, promoted, mentored, and championed ready? OnBoard looked around and discovered that the number of women who were moving up in corporations was rising, though not very quickly. Also, the number of very capable women in senior roles didn't necessarily know how to raise their hand for a board seat. What exactly should they do?

OnBoard's executive director, Rona Wells, developed a program to help women get ready for board service. She discovered that the mechanics of governance were familiar to the women in the group, and that the gaps they had in knowledge were easily remedied. What was more daunting was self-promotion. Recognizing the psychological aspects of "tooting one's own horn," Wells asked me to join her in helping the women in the group.

The issue in promoting oneself is not merely being noticed, but getting noticed for the things that are an advantage to your audience. Promotion in this case is not self-serving; rather, it is serving a mutual interest.

Understanding that is not difficult, but taking action on it is not so easy. Whether through the OnBoard Development Group, or other means, the organization has helped seventeen women land board seats. That number is likely to be more than twenty by the time this book is published.

Whether we are pursuing a corporate or a personal goal, when we set our sights on it, the risk of failure often looms before us. The pursuit may have the quality of very high stakes. These range from loss of revenue to loss of personal reputation—and everything in between. Fortitude, applied in a refined and disciplined manner, is a lever that we can use to reverse that risk.

Notes

1. Clayton M. Christensen, Richard Alton, Curtis Rising, and Andrew Waldeck, "The Big Idea: The New M&A Playbook," March 2011, accessed February 15, 2017, https://hbr.org/2011/03/the-big-idea-the-new-ma-playbook.
2. Scott A. Christofferson, Robert S. McNish, and Diane L. Sias, "Where Mergers Go Wrong," *McKinsey Quarterly*, May 2004, accessed February 15, 2017, www.mckinsey.com/business-functions/strategy-and-corporate-finance/our-insights/where-mergers-go-wrong.
3. "Making an Impact by the Numbers," *Onboard*, 2016, accessed February 15, 2017, www.onboardnow.org/wp-content/uploads/2016/11/OnBoard-Making-an-Impact.pdf.

CHAPTER 10

Truth

Up to this point in our exploration of leadership, the topic of honesty has not been directly addressed. It deserves some discussion as an important facet of fortitude, even though most people think of it as a character trait. This is only partly true, however, and this oversimplification is not useful.

Scientific research on the topic of honesty shows results similar to those on cognition, perception, and decision making. That is, we tend to think the behavior of *others* (especially bad or ill advised) is the result of an individual flaw, but what *we* do is more influenced by circumstance. Precisely because context is powerful, leaders need to keep a close eye on the environment of their organization. The culture of an organization is powerful precisely because it makes particular behaviors more or less likely and, collectively, strengthens beliefs about what is right and proper.

How does a leader influence effectively while maintaining an ethic of honesty? How easy is it to move the goal post from "not the whole truth" to "a bit of a lie"? Researcher and author Dan Ariely calls this the "fudge factor." It's telling a small lie, padding data, or making small adjustments in a calculation so it fits a belief. In his research at Duke University, Ariely has discovered that most everyone lies. Fortunately, most of us don't lie about big things. Only a few of us are systematically lying to gain an advantage at the expense of others. Bernie Madoff is one disheartening example. Yet, the number of small lies people tell, when taken together, can be as harmful as a big lie. The likelihood that someone will lie increases when he is able to rationalize and ignore the possible harm from the lie. Further, it is easier for people to engage in dishonest behavior when an entity—a business, a government agency, a nonprofit organization—sustains the harm of a lie, rather than an individual.

In mergers and acquisitions, each party presents itself in the best possible light, thus my comparison to courting.[1] When interviewing for a job, candidates are smart to understand the role and context, and to frame what they say to highlight why they are a good fit for the position. Representing a business with effective marketing means making particular elements of a product or service more visible than others. In each of these scenarios, we seek to influence others. We are not revealing the whole truth, nor is it expected that we would do so. Influence, as defined and described by Robert Cialdini, is not the same as deceit and lying.

When the stakes are high—and particularly in a crisis—people are more susceptible to social pressure. This is especially true when the "others" are like us or are in positions to which we aspire. This creates pressure to do things, even if we feel uneasy about these actions.

In 2007, after twenty-eight years as the dean of admissions at MIT, Marilee Jones was found to have lied about her academic background. The irony of lying about one's academic credentials to join an admissions office is not lost on anyone. Yet, as she moved up the organization—eventually to the head of the department—Jones kept quiet. A curious thing about lying is how quickly we minimize its seriousness in our own minds. In Jones's case, this lie perhaps seemed trivial in light of the quality of the work she did and the accolades she received for her success.

Surely, a lie on a résumé that was twenty-eight years old would pale in comparison to her achievements, right? Actually, it made things worse—much worse. Knowing that someone has been deceitful for a long time makes that person look worse to us. However, the opposite is the case from the person's own perspective. Why?

The first dishonest act is usually more troubling than the fifth or fiftieth. We adapt to the stories we tell in emotional and physical ways. A lie repeated—or one that we allow to be repeated on our behalf—becomes less potent to us. For others, it is the opposite. When we discover that someone else has been deceitful for a long period of time, we see it as evidence of a bad character flaw—perhaps an irredeemable one. Yet, sometimes it is the cover-up of a single deception rather than continuous wrongdoing that leads to downfall.

When a lie is out in the open and in the public domain, there are but two choices. One, confess and look for a way to repair the damage, or two, keep it up. Choice number two is tantalizing, as it involves avoidance of pain. The problem is, as Sir Walter Scott, famously wrote, "O, what a tangled web we weave when first we practice to deceive!"

Telling the Truth

Fred Sievert, the former chief executive officer of New York Life, says he had the good fortune to be raised by a mother who instilled in him the ethic of "doing the right thing." He also says that we must be willing to give up the idea that we know what the right thing is once we have more, and perhaps better, information. This sounds like a simple thing. However, once we understand the powerful need to preserve our own point of view, even if it takes selectively allowing new information to influence us, we can appreciate the value of Sievert's discipline.

While an executive at New York Life, but before he was CEO, Sievert took note of a disturbing fact. The long-term disability insurance product was losing money for the company. This product is an important risk-management tool and agents could honestly recommend it to clients for that reason. It also had a handsome commission structure attached to it. For these reasons, it was selling very well. As Sievert looked at the issue more closely, he did find a "few bad apples" in the barrel, that is, agents who were not entirely scrupulous in representing the product.

The solution? Sievert and his colleagues removed employees whose practices violated the values of the firm. This was a necessary first step, but Sievert believed the company should exit the business of selling long-term disability insurance altogether. As you might imagine, taking an action of this magnitude is a big decision for any company, and is especially difficult when the sales force is happy to have it available.

Sievert began talking about this issue with his colleagues and sharing hard financial data and other information he was collecting. As is his way, Sievert does a lot of work to pave the way for major decisions. If he thinks something needs to change, he works hard to get others on board by sharing information with them, again and again. Not satisfied to look backward, he communicates the impact of continuing a particular course of action, drawing it out for others. He realizes that sometimes an issue can look relatively minor in the present, but will become monumental if it is not corrected.

This was high stakes. If the leadership team did nothing, this product would hurt the company more over time. If the company stopped selling the product, the agents would be upset. Though Sievert had a strong conviction about what should be done, he didn't start off by telling his colleagues what to do. Gradually, he persuaded his colleagues to his point of view. Now, how would they break it to the agents who made up the company's sales force?

Sievert did a couple of things, the effectiveness of which was enhanced by his determined, steady style. *Fortitude* is a great word to describe Sievert, for more reasons that I can recount here. In any case, he tells his stories well in his book *God Revealed*. I know you are wondering how the former CEO of New York Life came to write a book with that title. He tells the reader better than I could.

First, Sievert spent time traveling around, talking with agents and others in the company. He came to understand how important the long-term disability product was as a tool for agents to help clients, and how significant it was for agents in building their own financial security. These things need not be mutually exclusive. The conversations he had gave Sievert a perspective that helped him to be empathetic to the agents' situation. That made him realize that he couldn't just convince the decision makers, he had to get the agents to accept this change by offering them something in return.

Sievert found another product the agents could offer instead of what they had been selling. This helped them continue to meet an important need of their clients, rather than cede the business to a competitor. And it allowed New York Life to exit this money-losing business without abandoning the agents. Fundamental to his ability to make this happen was his ethic of "doing the right thing." For Sievert, this means doing right by as many people as possible.

Running Toward Risk

Susan Packard, a cofounder of HGTV, took a risk when she and her colleagues launched the now phenomenally successful network. As in all new businesses, the risk is not singular but rather multiple, and of different types. In entertainment, the risks associated with talent are enormous. Can you get the people you need and want? What will it cost to get them? Will they perform in their job? Are they scandal prone? How will your financial backers react to the talent you assemble and to the way they perform and behave?

This issue may be more obvious in an entertainment environment, but it is no less important in other businesses. One of the most damaging mistakes I have seen in my work as a consultant is the tendency for leaders to avoid problems with people. Sometimes a very smart leader, capable in many ways, can be utterly unsure about how to handle an issue involving an individual. This is particularly true if the person is delivering strong results. The fear of loss is a powerful incentive to avoid facing a difficult situation.

Packard faced people-related dilemmas more than once in her career, notably when a very popular star was discovered to have falsified his résumé. But, for Packard, the decision was easy—the network's superstar was let go. Packard says that, as a leader, your behavior must tell people that you mean what you say. She says that sometimes leaders or superstars can drift into thinking that they get to play by a different set of rules than everyone else. If a leader allows it, she loses credibility in a big way.

Facing up to and dealing with a serious issue is what I mean by "running toward risk." Merely acknowledging it with a wait-and-see approach takes zero fortitude.

First, when a leader runs toward risk, she takes action. The leader looks for better information, whether she sees it firsthand or through the eyes of a third party. Either way, she finds a way to cut through organizational layers.

Second, the leader determines what is pertinent. When things go wrong, there is a great tendency for information to be voluminous but not necessarily valuable. A leader must distinguish noise from what is essential.

Third, the leader must make a decision. At any of these points, a leader can stall, but it is at this third point that negotiating with oneself is the most dangerous. This is when the human mind can lead us to rationalize— especially if we believe we can avoid discomfort.

The CEO of one of the largest charitable organizations in the United States spoke with me about a senior leader in his company. The senior leader was, to put it mildly, obnoxious. He brought a lot of money into the organization, but was rude and condescending to his colleagues, whom he openly stated were "C players."

The CEO felt stuck because he didn't want to run this person off, but things were becoming untenable. He asked me if the executive should have a coach, to which I replied, "Perhaps. But unless you address the problems, nothing will change, regardless." The CEO allowed this behavior for obvious reasons. Once I learned that the CEO didn't have the courage to deal with the situation directly, and that the executive was asking for more money, I found a solution. The CEO could tell the executive that his pay would increase only if he agreed to leave the organization and become a consultant. That worked.

You may be reading this and thinking that this CEO was a bad guy, weak and ineffective. That is not correct. He has had a distinguished career and he attracts very accomplished and internationally known people to the board. The organization has grown in size and reputation. He did have a weakness when it came to issues such as this, but here is the important thing: he knew it.

To ask for advice and help is neither weak nor is it evidence of a lack of fortitude. It is a valid action. Fortitude is about taking action in pursuit of one's objectives. Seeking advice in service of an objective is far from weak, as long as the leader is clear about the objectives. Henry Kissinger, speaking about presidential advisors on a Sunday morning news show, once said, "The president has to have some core convictions, he can't get those from advisors."[2] This is true of any leader, whether in business, government, or the nonprofit sector, and is especially true in a high-stakes situation, something with which Kissinger has deep knowledge.

While Susan Packard took a direct route to address an issue with a key person on her team, and the CEO who asked for my advice took a different route, each demonstrated fortitude. Conversely, John Stumpf—former CEO of Wells Fargo—sidestepped when he began to learn of the issues in the retail side of the company. He did not inform the board about the problems, even as they mounted. As we now know, the problems were significant and cost Wells Fargo tremendously, both in money and reputation lost. Stumpf resigned not only from his lucrative job at the bank, but also from the boards of Chevron and Target.

Ethics and Fortitude

What prevents someone from recognizing when they are rationalizing rather than using fortitude to face risk? Sometimes it is pure malice. Just as in Dan Ariely's research, some people are calculating and callous about the harm their schemes cause, but those are the minority of cases. The losses from such major failures as Tyco, WorldCom, Countrywide, Enron, and others are great, even if the perpetrators were few. In these cases, the leaders surely failed, but so did those who could have held them to account. A board of directors must have a level of fortitude at least equal to those in top management. Absent that, an unscrupulous leader—especially when in cahoots with his chief financial officer—can run amok.

While these few bad actors can cause major damage, most losses come from people who commit small acts of dishonesty such as cheating on taxes, cheating an insurance company, cheating small businesses, and a practice called "wardrobing." This last one requires explanation. It is a practice whereby people return clothing they have used. A consulting firm, in 2002, estimated this loss to be $16 billion. The people doing these things most assuredly consider themselves ethical and not susceptible to environmental influence.

Many years ago, a friend shocked me by telling me that she had purchased two fancy dresses for a single event. She wore one, then returned it to the store. She kept the second dress. I was really surprised because I had never known someone who did this with such aplomb, and certainly not someone who took great pride in her honesty. When I expressed shock to her about what she had done, my friend explained that "people do this all the time." Her mother had owned a clothing store and was aware of how often this happened. Rather than sensitize my friend to the harm caused by this practice, it made the behavior seem normal to her.

Because people are susceptible to environmental influence, leaders can influence the behavior of many people at one time. Often, attempts to do this begin with statements of values. That's fine so far as it goes, but it is far from enough. Leaders need to say what they expect and provide specifics as well as generalities. Saying "we believe in integrity" is fine. Sure, who doesn't? It's much better to say, "We demonstrate integrity by _____."

When leaders show a lack of fortitude in facing dishonesty—especially when the person committing the dishonest acts is valuable or popular—it undermines the leader and sets up an obvious double standard. As important as honesty and integrity are for a leader, fairness is a close third. People are less invested and less happy when the leader's decisions seem unfair.

The employees of Wells Fargo who were fired for failing to open a sufficient number of new accounts have every cause to feel they were treated unfairly. After the disaster became public, the bank posted full-page ads in national newspapers and sent letters to customers. The text was apologetic but unconvincing.

When crises like this happen in an organization, more needs to happen than saying "sorry," like a recalcitrant two-year-old. A board needs to take a serious look at the business, starting with its leaders. If leaders say one thing and do another, or say one thing and allow others to do the opposite, they will eventually reap the bitter results.

Auditors and compliance people will continue to look for wrongdoing. Leaders should be in the business of preventing bad behavior by being exemplars of good behavior. The first and most important thing for leaders to do if they want to see forthrightness in others is to display it themselves. There is no substitute.

Notes

1. Constance R. Dierickx, "Invisible Rip Tides Sink Mergers and Marriages," *CD Consulting Group*, updated July 2015, www.cdconsultinggrp.com/resources/ articles/invisible-rip-tides-sink-mergers-and-marriages/.
2. Henry Kissinger, "Interview on *Face the Nation*," CBS, December 18, 2016, accessed February 15, 2017, www.cbsnews.com/videos/interview-henry-kiss inger-december-18/.

CHAPTER 11

High-Stakes Leaders of the Future

The leaders with whom I have worked over the years think and talk a lot about how to help others acquire leadership skills. Surprisingly, they rarely ask me about how to help people become better in technical ways. This isn't because technical knowledge isn't valuable; it is. Indeed, ignoring changes of a technical nature will truly come back to haunt businesses, nonprofit organizations, and individuals. Technical changes present avenues of leverage and great risk.

Technology has enabled businesses to expand in ways we couldn't have imagined a few years ago. It has also allowed thieves access to assets without ever leaving their own homes—just ask any leader of a company whose computer systems have been hacked, or any individual who has been scammed out of his life savings by someone he knows only in a virtual world. The reason leaders think and talk about leadership skills is that they are much rarer than technical skills. Even more rare is the combination of knowledge, leadership skills, and strong character.

A key job of every leader is to find, teach, and develop those who can take over when he moves on. To do this well takes courage, judgment, and fortitude.

Flexibility and Inclination

It is striking that what makes a good leader today is not substantially different than what was required to be a good leader years or even decades ago. The context within which anyone leads may vary widely depending on industry, geography, and time, but the characteristics of good leaders are remarkably consistent. Yet, the selection of leaders often overuses criteria that comfort those doing the selecting and don't necessarily result in the best outcomes. Typically, these criteria are track record and similarity.

What an individual has done may be impressive, but without understanding the context in which they did it, you don't really know whether or not his skills will be transferable to your organization. When Bob Nardelli left GE for The Home Depot, he had a solid track record, but in a very different business. Does that mean he couldn't have been successful in the new role or that anyone cannot? Of course not, but Nardelli's story offers an example of how important it is to ascertain whether someone has the flexibility and inclination to learn first and act second. There is no need to kick in the door with your gun drawn when a less intrusive leadership style will get you where you want to go.

Some will say that Nardelli was brought to The Home Depot precisely to make changes. Great. All the more reason to understand how he got the results he had in the past. The problem with success is that it can lead us to think we have uncovered an immutable principle rather than a specific technique. It is equally easy to ignore the power of context. The very specific culture at GE helps the company implement all manner of strategy. The culture of The Home Depot was at the time, and is today, not conducive to the specific actions that Nardelli relied upon from his GE days.

If a new leader is to be successful in a business that is very different from the one in which he came, the likelihood of success is greatly increased by using principles illuminated by Robert Cialdini's research. One of these principles is to make people aware of change before you introduce a specific change. Talk about it, and use sayings that are either familiar or will quickly become so. Before this type of approach can work, the leader must have the flexibility and inclination to use influence before issuing directives or edicts.

The other highly influential aspect of choosing leaders is their similarity to people making the decision. This part of decision making is harder to detect because much of it operates outside of awareness. Our level of comfort is something we sense but don't usually question if it is high. If someone makes us uncomfortable, we can give lots of reasons and justifications for why that is. My very first consulting engagement happened in part because I had the right wardrobe. At the time, the pool of candidates was made up of doctoral candidates in a psychology program. The consulting client was AT&T, and the suits from my days as a stockbroker came in handy.

Later, when I worked with a client on CEO succession for the first time, no one questioned that I'd been in a boardroom many times. I hadn't. My age and wardrobe made the clients feel more comfortable because I was similar to the board members in appearance. It worked—though not just because I had the clothes. I had the ability to help them and the inclination to learn about my client before I fired off opinions.

Similarity can be used to influence for mutual gain or to take advantage. You need to discern whether the flexibility and inclination are directed in a way that is constructive or whether they are intended to put others at a disadvantage. A masterful portrayal of influence gone wrong is Will Smith's character in the film *Six Degrees of Separation*. Watching this character dupe others, who believe themselves to be sophisticated, illuminates an important principle. Similarity can easily be a stepping-stone to trust, even before it is justified.

Character—the Nonnegotiable

Previous chapters have highlighted leaders whose character I esteem. Virginia Hepner—CEO of the Woodruff Arts Center in Atlanta—is an exemplar. When faced with challenging circumstances, she relies upon her usual forthrightness to keep others informed, chart a path forward, and retain trust. Her ability to shoot straight, even when giving bad news, enhances her credibility. Credibility without solid character is merely a storyline that will quickly be understood as fiction.

Frank Blake, former CEO at The Home Depot, is another example of a leader with admirable character, as is Fred Sievert, former CEO of New York Life, and Susan Packard of HGTV. Leaders with character make tough decisions using principles of ethics, and can explain their thinking. They show an appreciation for the context and, far from being harsh, they recognize the hardships that will occur as a result of their decisions. They make an effort to find what I've coined the Triple Play, which I learned about from Susan Nethero, another leader described in this book.

Leaders with strong and admirable character understand not only the immediate consequences of their actions but also the longer-term results as well, including those that are intangible. Reputation of an organization, for example, is either an asset or a risk. Strong leaders understand that their personal reputation is entwined with that of their organization.

Even experienced leaders can make mistakes in hiring or promoting those who later reveal a lack of character that is disheartening and embarrassing. If this happens, it's best to face it, admit it, make the corrections possible, and move on. It sounds easy, but the urge to save face can be strong and lead people down the path of rationalization. If you find yourself explaining away behavior that concerns you, it's best to ask if you are avoiding unpleasantness when it ought to be dealt with.

Many leaders ask how they can tell if someone has good character. There are a few ways to look at a person that can reduce the risk of misjudging. It is most important that you consider these, especially when you are extremely confident!

For example, do you know of some situations in which the person faced a difficult and ambiguous situation? What did he do, and how does he explain it? I find that people who have a higher-than-justified opinion of their own ethical core will give examples that are challenging but not ambiguous. Stories of letting someone go for stealing, for example, are clear and not at all ambiguous. It is far more challenging when the objectionable act is up for interpretation, or if the behavior is in dispute. Everyone has had an experience where he needed to use judgment to make a decision in circumstances where the right answer wasn't obvious or there is no right answer. When thinking about a specific person and situation, you want to know:

- Is the person courageous in facing reality?
- Is his judgment solid?
- Does she have the fortitude to act?

Sharks

I really like two TV shows featuring successful entrepreneurs, *Shark Tank* and *The Profit*. I wrote about Marcus Lamonis earlier because he exemplifies many of the attributes this book applauds. He and those on *Shark Tank* have some things in common.

First, they have a discipline about how they look at a business, how they make investment decisions, and what advice they give to aspiring entrepreneurs. They love a good story, but if reality doesn't match, they are quick to point out that the facts don't support the story. Passion and enthusiasm are great, but on their own they don't justify an investment. Neither does a good idea without an enthusiastic potential partner. The courage to apply your own principles (not techniques or tactics) is fundamental. The principles used by each shark are augmented by his or her knowledge of the larger context. Listen to the sharks talk about trends, markets, and demographic shifts. They are not applying their principles in an echo chamber. Rather, they have an awareness of the larger, global context. Leaders of the future must have this same awareness and drive.

Second, the entrepreneurs have a firm grasp of what they are good at, what they know. They also know when a pitch is for something they don't know much or anything about. They will back away from something that requires competencies they do not possess. Their judgment about their own strengths is solid.

Finally, they have the fortitude to act. They decide and make a call—go or no go—on each possible investment. If they do the deal, they follow through with support and advice for their new partners and demand the same fortitude from them. Watch Marcus Lamonis when he confronts people about their level of commitment. He is extremely direct. Some people walk away and others thrive when they have a partner like Lamonis.

The shows are fun and the lessons valid. However, the stars of these shows have an advantage over the leaders I know and work with. What is that? They are unencumbered by history and relationships. The shows are laboratories that provide a way for us to learn as well as to be entertained. But make no mistake, leaders cannot ignore the context in which they operate.

Drive to Learn

A prominent attribute of many good leaders—and successful people—is curiosity. Curiosity is what underlies breadth of knowledge that, in turn, allows a person to mentally create many more permutations than someone without it. Think of it as playing Scrabble with a very large vocabulary rather than a limited one. The possibilities expand exponentially. Mark Cuban, technology entrepreneur and owner of the Dallas Mavericks, is a constant learner. He pokes his head into anything that looks interesting or might be an opportunity. This got him fired, but also got him fired up enough to realize that he couldn't work for someone else. Perhaps he could have, but not someone who was envious of his drive and capability.

Charlie Munger, longtime colleague and confidant of Warren Buffett, uses the term *learning machine*—people who "go to bed every night a little wiser than they were when they got up."[1] He describes Buffet as a learning machine, but the description fits Munger as well. His knowledge of investing is as deep as you would expect. What you might not know is the breadth of his knowledge and his commitment to learn continuously. Viewing his commencement speech at the USC School of Law is a deep dive into wisdom, though I doubt he would agree. His focus is on what he will learn next, as he believes that "wisdom acquisition is a moral duty."[2] He states that the performance of Berkshire Hathaway, surely one of the most admired and successful companies to ever exist, would be impossible were it not for the constant learning of Warren Buffett.

To be a constant learner—or, as Munger says, a learning machine—takes courage, judgment, and fortitude. I would argue that people who consume information from mediocre sources may be learning in the strictest sense but not advancing their ability to think. It takes courage to read and to study ideas that have no obvious value, such as the classics. It takes judgment and fortitude to decide to ignore organizational gossip or the streams of blather on social media or talk radio.

Learning that leads to wisdom and insight comes from the hard work of personal experience. Reading and exploring for oneself rather than taking the word of others means effort over sloth. You may recall the story of my client who came very close to firing the CEO based on a rumor. Upon further investigation, I discovered that the rumor was not only baseless, but also motivated by a malevolent board member.

Regardless, the rumor caught fire in the minds of those who were his allies but who lacked the courage to question his report or the initiative to learn the facts. It became a crisis that, fortunately, was brought to an end by some fresh air and light of day. There was long-term damage to some key relationships as a result, and the nastiness leaked out, as it usually does. This was a costly misstep, and it came at a time when the board and new CEO were on stage.

While this situation became a crisis, it was short lived. The board asked for help and, in quick order, the issue was sorted. Board members were embarrassed but came clean. Individuals admitted their mistakes and took accountability. One offered to resign. The CEO and most of the board members were able to work together for several years afterward, and those who were disgruntled became cooperative, if not enthusiastic.

It took the courage, judgment, and fortitude of participants for this to happen. Those who had these characteristics to start with influenced the others in a positive way, and in the end, the leadership came together in the best interests of the company.

Afterward, some remarked that the situation had become far more difficult than was necessary. Yet, the board members couldn't see their way out of the downward spiral on their own. True, some of the people involved didn't behave well, by their own admission. When people are involved, things can get messy because we are dealing with both the manifest issues and those beneath the surface. Smart, well-intended people derail and can appear irrational, unreasonable, and petty.

It may seem logical to separate the people in this or any scenario according to who behaved badly and who behaved well. That is part of the criteria but not all of it. After a debacle such as this, an opportunity awaits. Those who were involved and behaved well—but were happy to remain bystanders— may not be the leaders you seek. On the other side, those you labeled troublemakers may have value to contribute. It's a mistake to focus only on those who disappointed you. Find out who has the drive to learn. This is an asset.

Speed of Change

As many have noted, the speed at which things are changing in the world around us has accelerated considerably over the past few decades. I joked with a similar-age friend upon seeing the Apple Watch for the first time that his was way beyond what Dick Tracy ever had or imagined. Even for a kid who grew up less than ten miles from Cape Canaveral and the pulsing heart of America's space program, our world has changed dramatically. Information moves quickly, and fake news just as quickly. One could sit in front of a computer all day and consume all manner of knowledge, wisdom— and pure garbage. What keeps us from taking in mind-numbing or mind-polluting content? What allows a leader to sort through massive amounts of data, knowing in advance that it is of unequal value?

Judgment, and the courage and the fortitude to use it.

Absent the discernment that arises from judgment, we are like the shiny silver balls in a pinball machine, subject to forces outside our control and helpless to get where we want to go because of the action of levers and rebounders. Sad to say, but many executives feel a level of helplessness about their schedules, as they are in response mode more often than not. Meeting after meeting drives an internal focus that leaves them less able to anticipate shifts in the market and out of touch with customers.

The irony is, the more change exists in the external environment, the greater the need for leaders to turn toward it. Inward focus leads to commiserating about changes coming from external sources but little capacity to anticipate it and no ability to cause it.

High-stakes leaders must be tuned in to the environment in as many aspects as humanly possible. This can happen in two ways: first, by personal connection with the external environment, and second, by reading. The knowledge one acquires from each builds upon itself and the other. Knowledge does more than accumulate; a knowledgeable person can become aware of how she learns. This is a breakthrough for anyone, especially when change accelerates, and it is even more critical if you intend to create the change that you want to see in your organization—and in the world.

Your Future Self

When I was young, I thought of knowledge like a library—it fell into categorized sections, like books and periodicals did. If you were in the mathematics section and wanted to read something about geography, you had to physically move. First, you had to go to the place that would tell you where the geography books were and then you had to walk to them. I thought it was important to choose an area and dig in. This was deeply frustrating because I didn't know which one to choose.

Then, in high school, I took a class in sociology and another in logic. Yes, this was high school. I was lucky to attend a public school where we could learn these things, and read Shakespeare and dissect sharks in marine biology. Of course, I didn't realize the advantage until later. Still, I couldn't quite get away from the library analogy.

Then I met the first person whom I thought was a real scholar—a college professor. I realized that knowledge becomes wisdom only when it is both deep and broad. His ability to mentally access multiple domains was a revelation. This was a neural network, not a filing cabinet.

This sort of thinking about thinking, or metacognition, is important in high-stakes situations, but is also useful in general if one desires fulfillment. Two key aspects of metacognition are knowledge and regulation. That is, *what* do you know, and *how* and *when* do you apply it? What we know is the part that gets a lot of attention, but on its own it's not enough to make you a good leader. How you apply what you know is necessary, as is a third piece: *Why* are you doing it?

If you don't know why you want to lead, it's a good question to ponder. I frequently meet with very senior leaders who don't have a clear picture of why they want to lead. They are usually smart, very motivated, memorable, and socially skillful. They have achieved a level of financial success that secures not only their own future, but also that of the next generation of their family. Yet, they don't always know why they are doing what they are doing beyond fulfilling an organizational strategy and their own ambition. As leaders become aware of this, it often nags at them. Yet, it isn't so easy to talk about even though it is important.

Ask yourself: What is my purpose? What do I stand for? What difference does my leadership make? Your answers to these very important questions will help guide your future self—whether within your current organization and career path, or toward something altogether different.

Accelerate

The question I'm often asked is, "Now what?" Meaning, now that we have had a discussion of ideas, what actions should we take?

The answer is always the same and always frustrates because it is conceptual. The right decisions are discovered, not retrieved from a vending machine.

If you are serious about leadership and are drawn to high-stakes situations, ask yourself the questions that follow. If you are serious about leadership but are *not* drawn to high-stakes situations, keep reading anyway. High-stakes situations and crises will arise whether or not you seek them out. In a crisis, people look to the leader for direction. If the leader doesn't provide it, someone will step into the vacuum. Will you lead or stand back while someone else does? Either way, don't let the answer be an abdication. Make it a decision.

Considering the following statements will help you understand where to spend your energy.

Courage

1. I have a purpose for what I do that is greater than my own reward.
2. I stop others who are veering off course.
3. I will voice an unpopular opinion without hostility.
4. I let people know when they have failed to perform as agreed.
5. I remove people who are not effective and who fail to accept responsibility.
6. I hold myself accountable.
7. I admit mistakes and apologize to those who are inconvenienced or harmed.
8. I am intentional about learning broadly and continuously.
9. I take action to fill in my own gaps in knowledge.
10. I am more curious than judgmental.

Judgment

1. I get to the core of complex problems.
2. I anticipate consequences and plan for them.
3. I tune out feedback that I didn't ask for or from those I do not respect.
4. I recognize when someone is a "yes person."
5. I eschew perfection.
6. I take the long view.
7. I separate the important from the unimportant.
8. I know that reaching out for help is a sign of strength.
9. I avoid using rumor as the basis of decisions.
10. I believe that how things are done has consequences as large as what is done.

Fortitude

1. I am resilient in the face of setbacks.
2. I have confidence in my ability to figure things out.
3. I get to know what others want, what they are good at, and how it fits in.
4. I will assertively take control of a conversation to get to the point.

5. I do not promote people unless they are performing *and* continuously growing and learning.
6. I put in the work necessary, but not more than necessary.
7. I look for innovative ideas in traditional and unexpected places.
8. I am responsible for my own growth and development.
9. I have confidence that I can acquire new skills.
10. I give up only when the objective no longer makes sense.

Create Your Plan

Now that you have considered the previous statements, and perhaps a few of your own, create a plan. Give yourself thirty minutes, and do it. You can change it later, but if you labor over this part you'll lose energy. Doing it quickly will create energy.

What is my objective? The answer to this should be in the form of an outcome. It should answer the question: what will be different?

What good will achieving my objectives do? For whom? Make sure that your objectives are actually going to have the outcomes that you want, and that they serve the people they should.

What do I currently have that will help me achieve my most important objective? Consider skills, knowledge, relationships, reputation, and so forth Look to past successes and what you drew upon to achieve them.

What is the greatest barrier to me achieving my most important objective? Look to past events where you stumbled and ask why. Don't let yourself off the hook, but don't beat yourself up either.

Of those things that will help me achieve my goals, which do I love doing that I am also great at? The combination of talent and passion is a winning one. Are you in the right place to put this to use? If not, what will you do about that? If you are, go for it!

Notes

1. Vladimir Oane, "Hacking Your Way to Becoming a Learning Machine," *Vladimir Says* [blog], June 25, 2015, accessed February 15, 2017, http://vladimir says.com/blog/2015/6/25/hacking-my-way-to-becoming-a-learning-machine.
2. Elena Holodny, "29 Brilliant Quotes From Charlie Munger, Warren Buffett's Right-Hand Man," October 1, 2014, accessed February 15, 2017, Ibid. www. businessinsider.com/charlie-mungers-best-quotes-2014-9?op=1.

CONCLUSION

The Highest Stakes of All

Throughout this book, I have described leaders at the top of different types of organizations—large and small, as well as publicly owned, privately held, and not-for-profit. This was a deliberate choice, made so that you, the reader, could see the commonality among leaders who rise to the challenges of high-stakes situations—as well as among those leaders who do not. Further, you can see that assuming the calm of the status quo will continue unabated is a foolish dream, but it's one we can be lulled into.

There is a significant benefit to being in a high-stakes situation when it is obvious that the stakes are elevated. A crisis or looming challenge makes us alert. Of course, that does not mean our readiness will be equal to the events. That is precisely why judgment is so important. Conversely, a lack of awareness fuels complacency and, in the extreme, smugness. Recalling the surprise attack at Pearl Harbor, a dramatic example, most people think that had they been involved, the attack wouldn't have happened. This is not true. The limitations of perception, judgment, and decision making are all part of being human. What of the scandals at Wells Fargo and VW? It is easy to read about these and shake our heads in disbelief. How did the leaders not know what was going on? Why do so many leaders treat matters such as these as primarily public relations problems? It is because they do not realize, or refuse to realize, how high the stakes actually are.

Not long after Berkshire Hathaway acquired a significant stake in Salomon Brothers, a scandal broke. What happened next is a case study in how valuable courage, judgment, and fortitude are when the stakes are high, and they were very high. Indeed, Salomon Brothers could have gone into bankruptcy, which would have, in turn, dealt a serious blow to Berkshire Hathaway. A detailed story of these events by Carol Loomis, longtime friend of Warren Buffet, is worth reading.[1] Immediately after the directors learned of the situation, Buffet was named interim chairman of the company and, characteristically, faced the situation with absolute intellectual honesty.

Facing difficult circumstances takes courage, deciding what to do takes judgment, and acting requires fortitude. Leaders who exemplify these qualities are everywhere, in businesses and organizations of all sizes, and often their talent prevents crises and high-stakes situations from developing in the first place.

Note

1. Carol Loomis, "Warren Buffet's Wild Ride at Solomon," *Fortune Magazine*, October 27, 1997, accessed February 18, 2017, http://fortune.com/1997/10/27/warren-buffett-salomon/.

References

Asch, Solomon E. "Opinions and Social Pressure." *Scientific American*, 193 (1955), 35.

Bierman, John. *Righteous Gentile*. New York: Penguin, 1996.

CD Consulting Group. "Invisible Rip Tides Sink Mergers and Marriages." Updated July 2015. www.cdconsultinggrp.com/resources/articles/invisible-rip-tides-sink-mergers-and-marriages/.

CD Consulting Group. "Vital Marketing Concepts to Grow a Business." www.youtube.com/watch?v=cXT-OxZgEV4.

Christensen, Clayton M., Richard Alton, Curtis Rising, and Andrew Waldeck. "The Big Idea: The New M&A Playbook." March 2011. Accessed February 15, 2017. https://hbr.org/2011/03/the-big-idea-the-new-ma-playbook.

Cialdini, Robert. *Influence, Science and Practice*. 5th Edition. Pearson, 2009.

Dean, Jeremy. "How Rewards Can Backfire and Reduce Motivation." *Psyblog*. October 2009. Accessed February 15, 2017. www.spring.org.uk/2009/10/how-rewards-can-backfire-and-reduce-motivation.php.

Dierickx, Constance. The Efficacy of a Culturally Tailored Intervention for HIV Prevention in Deaf Adults. 1998. Doctoral Dissertation.

Dierickx, Constance, and Linda Henman. "Deal or No Deal." Last Updated August 2016. www.cdconsultinggrp.com/wp-content/themes/cdconsult/pdf/Deal-or-No-Deal.pdf.

Dranikoff, Lee, Tim Koller, and Antoon Schneider. "Divestiture: Strategy's Missing Link." May 2005. Accessed February 15, 2017. https://hbr.org/2002/05/divestiture-strategys-missing-link.

Dweck, Carol. *Mindset: The New Psychology of Success*. New York: Random House, 2006.

Feynman, Richard P. "Report of the Presidential Commission on the Space Shuttle Challenger Accident. Volume 2: Appendix F—Personal Observations on Reliability of Shuttle." June 1986. Accessed February 15, 2017. http://history.nasa.gov/rogersrep/v2appf.htm.

Fisher, Jeffrey D., and William A. Fisher. "Changing AIDS-Risk Behavior." *Psychological Bulletin,* 111 (1992), 455–474.

Gibson, Elizabeth, and Andy Billings. *Big Change at Best Buy*. Nicholas Brealey Publishing, 2003.

Glazer, Emily. "How Wells Fargo's High-Pressure Sales Culture Spiraled Out of Control." *The Wall Street Journal*, September 16, 2016.

Grant, Adam. *Originals: How Non-Conformists Move the World*. New York: Viking, 2016.

Hesselbein, Frances. *My Life in Leadership: The Journey and Lessons Learned Along the Way*. Wiley, 2011.

Holodny, Elena. "29 Brilliant Quotes From Charlie Munger, Warren Buffett's Right-Hand Man." October 2014. Accessed February 15, 2017. Ibid. www.businessinsider.com/charlie-mungers-best-quotes-2014-9?op=1.

Kahneman, Daniel. *Thinking, Fast and Slow*. Farrar, Straus and Giroux, 2011.

Kissinger, Henry. "Interview." *Face the Nation*. CBS. December 18, 2016. Accessed February 15, 2017. www.cbsnews.com/videos/interview-henry-kissinger-december-18/.

Kotter, John. "Can You Handle an Exponential Rate of Change?" July 19, 2011. Accessed February 20, 2017. www.forbes.com/sites/johnkotter/2011/07/19/can-you-handle-an-exponential-rate-of-change/#309e4d5a1f6f.

Loomis, Carol. "Warren Buffet's Wild Ride at Solomon." *Fortune Magazine*. October 27, 1997. Accessed February 18, 2017. http://fortune.com/1997/10/27/warren-buffett-salomon/.

Milgram, Stanley. *Obedience to Authority: An Experimental View*. Reprint Edition. Harper Perennial Modern Classics, 2009.

Oane, Vladimir. "Hacking Your Way to Becoming a Learning Machine." *Vladimir Says* [blog]. June 25, 2015. Accessed February 15, 2017. http://vladimirsays.com/blog/2015/6/25/hacking-my-way-to-becoming-a-learning-machine.

Onboard. "Making an Impact, by the Numbers." 2016. Accessed February 15, 2017. www.onboardnow.org/wp-content/uploads/2016/11/On Board-Making-an-Impact.pdf.

Reingold, Jennifer. "How Home Depot CEO Frank Blake Kept His Legacy From Being Hacked." October 2014. Accessed February 15, 2017. http://fortune.com/2014/10/29/home-depot-cybersecurity-reputation-frank-blake/

Russo, J. Edward, and Paul J. H. Schoemaker. *Winning Decisions: Getting It Right the First Time.* New York: Doubleday, 2001.

Seligman, Martin. *Learned Optimism: How to Change Your Mind and Your Life.* New York: Free Press, 1990.

Taylor, Richard. "Time and Life's Meaning." *Review of Metaphysics,* 40 (1987), 675–686.

Thompson, Mark. "America: Meet Your First Female Rangers." August 20, 2015. Accessed February 15, 2017. http://time.com/4005578/female-army-rangers/.

Tversky, Amos, and Daniel Kahneman. "Judgment Under Uncertainty: Heuristics and Biases." *Science,* 185 (1974), 1124–1131.

Viorst, Judith. *Necessary Losses: The Loves, Illusions, Dependencies, and Impossible Expectations That All of Us Have to Give Up in Order to Grow.* Free Press, 1998.

Wells Fargo. "Our Values." Wells Fargo corporate website, Accessed February 15, 2017. www.wellsfargo.com/about/corporate/vision-and-values/our-values.

Wells Fargo. "Wells Fargo to Eliminate Product Sales Goals for Retail Bankers." September 13, 2016. Accessed February 15, 2017. www.wellsfargo.com/about/press/2016/eliminate-sales-goals_0913/.

Zimbardo, Phillip G., Christina Maslach, and Craig Haney. (2000). "Reflections on the Stanford prison experiment: Genesis, transformations, consequences." In Thomas Blass (Ed.), *Obedience to Authority: Current Perspectives on the Milgram Paradigm* (pp. 193–237). Mahwah, NJ: Erlbaum.

Index

About the Author

Constance Dierickx, PhD, specializes in working with organizations in high-stakes situations such as mergers, acquisitions, CEO succession, strategic change, and crisis. Known as "the secret weapon," she has worked with clients such as AT&T, Belk, Boys and Girls Clubs of America, Chubb, Darden Restaurants, IBM, Johnson Controls, NextGear Capital, Schnabel Engineering, and Westinghouse. Dierickx has advised more than five hundred executives on five continents in more than twenty industries.

Earlier in her career, Dierickx was a broker at Merrill Lynch, where she observed firsthand the power of emotion and perceptual distortion on major decisions. Her curiosity about the behavior of clients and colleagues led her to study psychology and decision making. She has been interviewed for the *Wall Street Journal, Fast Company, Fortune,* and *USA Today* and has written articles for publications such as *American Business Magazine, Boards and Directors, Corporate Board Member, Directorship,* and *Chief Executive* magazine.

Dierickx lives in Atlanta with her husband, Michael, a Certified Financial Planner™. An enthusiastic amateur chef and traveler, she also maintains an inexplicable interest in boxing.